SIGIL
AND TRANSFORMATION

111 Magick Sigils to Change
and Control Your Life

Adam Blackthorne

THE GALLERY OF
MAGICK

Copyright © 2016 Adam Blackthorne

All Rights Reserved. This book may not be reproduced, in whole or in part, in any form or by any means electronic or mechanical, including photocopying, recording, or by any information storage retrieval system now known or hereafter invented, without written permission from the publisher, The Gallery of Magick.

It is hereby expressly stated that the images in this book may not be reproduced in any form, except for individual and personal use. Derivative works based on these images are not permitted, and any such attempt to create a derivative work will be met with legal action.

Disclaimer: Consider all information in this book to be speculation and not professional advice, to be used at your own risk. Adam Blackthorne and The Gallery of Magick are not responsible for the consequences of your actions. The information is never intended to replace or substitute for psychological or medical advice from a professional practitioner, and when it comes to issues of physical health, mental health or emotional conditions, no advice is given or implied, and you should always seek conventional, professional advice. The information is provided on the understanding that you will use it in accordance with the laws of your country.

CONTENTS

The Power of the Sigils	11
The Nature of the Sigils	15
The Sigils of Creative Light	19
The Source of the Sigils	21
How to Use the Sigils	29
Sigils in Practice	41
The Flow of Magick	45
Emergency Magick	49
The Sigils and Their Powers	55

THE MAGICK OF THE MIND

Enhance Your Concentration	58
Increase Dream Recall	60
Understand the Messages in Dreams	62
Experience a Lucid Dream	64
Recover a Sense of Joy	66

INSPIRING OTHERS

Improve the Mood of Loved Ones	70
Improve the Mood of Those Around You	72
Uncover the Warmth in Others	74
Encourage Compassion	76
Encourage Understanding	78
Encourage Love	80
Encourage Trust	82
Encourage Change and Transformation	84

EXTENDED PERCEPTION

Uncover Secret Thoughts	88
Sense the Near Future	90

Sense the Far Future	92
Recover a Lost Object	94
Connect Psychically with Another	96

FORTUNE

Obtain a Fair Legal Decision	100
Be Seen in a Good Light	102
Thrive in Competition	104
Make a Good Decision	106
Be Given a Chance	108

LOVE AND FRIENDSHIP

Attract Worthy Friendship	112
Recover Lost Love	114
Attract Romance	116
Discover the Feelings of One You Care For	118
End a Relationship Peacefully	120
Become the Centre of Attention	122
Attract Love Over Long Distance	124
Maintain Love Over Long Distance	126
Embrace Your Loyalty	128
Renew Passion	130

BREAKTHROUGH MAGICK

Open the Road to New Opportunities	134
Discover Creative Talents	136
Improve Creative Inspiration	138
Welcome Intuition	140
Expand Available Time	142

SPIRITUAL MAGICK

Sense the Spiritual	146
Discover Your Spiritual Path	148
Discover Your Material Path	150

Find Wisdom in Problems 152
Discover Your True Passion 154

PERSONAL STRENGTH

Increase Willpower 158
Break a Habit 160
Overcome Procrastination 162
Find Relief from Addiction 164
Experience Self-Confidence 166
Finish What You Start 168

PEACE MAGICK

Obtain Peace and Balance 172
Silence the Negative Voice 174
Ease the Pain of Memories 176
Banish Guilt and Shame 178
End Bad Luck 180
Heal a Damaged Relationship 182
Heal a Damaged Friendship 184
Heal a Damaged Work Relationship 186
End an Argument Peacefully 188
Give Comfort and Peace 190

PROTECTION MAGICK

Banish Negative Energy 194
Cancel a Curse 196
Find a Pathway from Crisis 198
Protection Against Physical Violence 200
Protect Against Psychic Attack 202
Make Your Enemy Find Peace 204
Move from Anger to Peace 206
Remove Unwanted Attention 208
Discover Those Who Drain Your Energy 210
Ease People Out of Your Life 212

Make an Enemy Feel Compassion	214
Make an Enemy Sense Your Power	216
Bring Peace to a Home	218
Make Noisy Neighbors Quiet	220

PERSONAL HEALING

Overcome Anxiety	224
Banish Fear and Worry	226
Ease Depression	228
Quieten the Mind	230
Lighten Your Mood	232
Overcome Bitterness	234
Release the Pain of Jealousy	236

HEALTH MAGICK

Discover the Willpower to Eat Well	242
Reduce Your Appetite Through the Joy of Eating	244
Uncover The Motivation to Exercise	246
Find More Physical Energy	248
Heal Sore Bones and Joints	250
Recover from Stomach Sickness	252
Ease Chronic Pain	254
Cope with Symptoms	256
Recover Rapidly from Colds and Flu	258
Make Your Skin Glow with Health	260
Heal with Loving Light	262
Encourage Deep Sleep	264
Release the Energy of Youthfulness	266
Sharpen Your Mind	268

WISDOM AND EDUCATION

Learn with Ease	272
Pass Exams Easily	274
Develop a New Skill Easily	276

Improve Organizational Skills   278
Find a Great Teacher   280

BUSINESS AND FINANCE

Business Booster   284
Raise Money for Your Projects   286
Money from Out of the Blue   288
Steady Income Increase   290
Make Your Money Go Further   292
Enjoy Spending and Sharing   294

EMPLOYMENT MAGICK

Attract a Promotion   298
Attract a Job That Suits Your Needs   300
Perform Well at Interview   302
Be Noticed by People of Importance   304
Communicate Clearly   306
Communicate to a Group   308

End Notes   311

The Power of Sigils

There are no magick words in this book that can make you rich. There is no secret symbol that can bring you love. Calling on spirits, angels, and gods is not what we're doing here. Magick can be complicated, boring, mind-boggling or a total failure, but when you work with the sigils in this book, you throw out all the confusing magickal garbage and get straight to the power of change.

It's simple and direct, but the exciting truth is that magick does work. When you tap into the light of creation, using these powerful sigils, magick can bring you the things you want. Sigils provide you with a visual code that unlocks the essence of magick.

This book does not contain anything to do with witchcraft, spellcasting, kabbalistic ritual, evocation or any other method of magick that you might be familiar with. It is pure sigil magick, connecting your inner desires to the Creative Light of change. I'll explain what that means in plain English, before too long.

There are one hundred and eleven sigils in this book that can help with anything from self-confidence to luck, from healing to protection, and from inspiration and intuition to love. The subject areas covered here are *The Magick of the Mind, Inspiring Others, Extended Perception, Fortune, Love and Friendship, Breakthrough Magick, Spiritual Magick, Personal Strength, Peace Magick, Protection Magick, Personal Healing, Health Magick, Wisdom and Education, Business and Finance* and *Employment Magick*. You can scan through the table of contents to see how many powers and abilities and ways to change are on offer.

This book does not call on angels, demons or any spirits. The magick presented here is not bound to any religion, and it requires no magick words. You don't have to learn any difficult pronunciations or say a single word out loud. The magick requires no visualization and no equipment. You won't light a candle or wave a wand. All you need is this book, your own strong desire, and the will to carry out the instructions.

The magick works because you have access to one hundred and eleven secret sigils, handed down from ancient times. Every one of them can work wonders in the modern world.

A sigil is nothing more than a drawing, but in this case, the drawing is so much more than you can imagine. Sigils exist throughout magick and come in many different forms. Some sigils can be used to contact spirits, and we've published those in other books by The Gallery of Magick. Some sigils can be invented by the user, for a single, specific purpose – I covered that in *The Master Works of Chaos Magick*. The sigils in *this* book have a different history and a completely different application.

The history and origin of these sigils will be dipped into later in the book, ever so briefly, before we get to the practical magick. That's what you're here for – magick that works. But a tiny little magick history lesson is important, to let you see how and why these sigils are more than random doodles.

Sigils look like a bunch of squiggles wrapped up in a circle. They might look ordinary, like some crazy scribbling, or perhaps they make you shiver a little with a sense of magick. That's up to you. Whatever your first impression, these drawings bypass the conscious mind and connect you to a stream of Creative Light that has been channeled through the ages. You connect to a stream of success and prosperity that has been working in the background, bringing peace and happiness to many. If it sounds too good to be true, don't believe me, test it out. Ha! Everything we've *ever* said about magick in *every* book and blog post suggests you should never test the magick;

you should trust it. That is true. Usually. But if you're feeling skeptical, test run this magick on one problem. Not a huge problem. Test it on something that feels like it needs just a little extra shove to make it happen. But there's a catch! You can't test it in a half-hearted, cynical way. When you're doing the magick, you must follow my instructions to the letter, with full commitment and emotion. Do that, and the magick will work.

This is not dark magick, but magick of light. You can do no harm with this magick, to yourself or to others. If you succeed in business using this magick, it is not by bashing your competition into submission, but because you've made your business thrive in a way that makes it appeal to customers. If you succeed in love, it's not because you've drugged your would-be lover with spiritual confusion, but because you've opened up two hearts to the potential for love. It could be argued that any benefit to one is harm to another, but I think that's stretching the truth. From what I have seen, this magick is benign, harmless, kind - but effective. Call me a wishy-washy do-gooder if you want, but it's not my fault. That's just that nature of these particular sigils and the magick they connect you to. It's not all spiritual magick. There's plenty of material and financial magick too. Have a look at the table of contents. Whatever's going on in your life, you'll find something you need here.

The Nature of the Sigils

Now is the time to reveal this magick, for many reasons, and you could say that this book is my life's work. This is the magick that thrills me, and it's something I've been so eager to share with the world. I've spent a long, long time trying to get this book just right, so the images work exactly as they're meant to, and so you get the information you need to get it working, without a lot of pretentious babble and mystical waffle.

It could be said that no magick is truly hidden. We use the word 'secret' all the time, but magick is hidden in plain sight, and if you research thoroughly, and go through old documents, you will find all the secrets for yourself. The deeper secrets of magick are subtle and obscure, and it requires intelligence and patience to glean them from the old books, but the information is there if you buy a few hundred occult texts and work your way through them. You may fall asleep along the way because those ancient texts can be pretty dusty and pompous – but they contain all the amazing secrets that we share with you. Almost. There are some secrets that have not been shared so widely.

An important secret is how to apply the magick practically. That secret is hidden between the lines. It's hidden in private grimoires. It's passed from generation to generation, from person to person. And now, it's shared by modern occultists, in books. If you want to know how to make the magick work, the secrets can be found here. That is what I can do for you. In a few short chapters, you'll learn what you need to know because this is a secret I am downright thrilled to share with you.

I came from a background that could be politely described as humble (or more honestly described as 'living hell'), but I was lucky enough to discover this strand of magick, and it changed my life, just as it can change yours. Lots of magick has helped change my life, but these sigils contain an essence of magick that excites me the most. I have researched more magick than I ever guessed existed, from all over the world, and

I've used a *lot* of that magick, and it has been a fascinating adventure – I've tried a lot of crazy stuff along the way.

One thing I am certain of is that most magick works a bit, but most magick doesn't work as well as you want it to work. There are many styles and methods that *can* work, under certain circumstances, if you find a way to capture the right energy. There are loads of tricks that can get magick to work; personal energy, belief, emotion, willpower, imagination – hundreds of different ways. Magick can be made extremely simple, but lots of magick requires intense willpower, a perfect visual imagination, and a deep belief. Guess what? Not in this book! You don't need willpower, visual imagination, or belief. That's going to make life a lot easier for you.

You do work with desire, decision, and your will, but that's not the same thing as straining with willpower and belief. It's relatively effortless. That can be difficult to accept, I know. Every once in a while somebody reviews our books and says, 'You can't get something for nothing. It takes more effort than this.' As you can discover, that limiting belief is blissfully wrong.

You don't need to be a true believer or an occultist. You can be an ordinary person who does some magick, and the magick will work. For magick to work, it helps if there's a little sparkling sense of excitement that perhaps - just maybe - magick might work. If you sense that there's a supernatural reality, beyond the ordinary world, that's all you need. Oh, and one other thing. You need to read everything in this book and follow the instructions exactly. That means *all* the instructions.

It's going to be so much easier than you expect, but just because it's simple doesn't mean it can be slapdash or half-hearted. If you want it to work, do it properly. I'm one of those people who buys a new camera and plays with it for a few weeks before getting out the instruction manual and realizing that, oh, yeah, it's actually really easy to use, and you can take such great pictures if you know how to use the settings. I should know better. *Get the instruction manual out first!* That means, read the instructions until you understand them. Then do the magick. The good news: I bet that's going to take less than an hour. If you don't have an hour to spare to learn magick, you don't really deserve to learn magick. Harsh, but fair.

Some of the chapter titles in this book are identical, or almost identical to chapter titles in other books published by The Gallery of Magick, such as Damon Brand's *Words of Power*. In this book there's a ritual called, *Make Your Money Go Further*, just like in *Words of Power*. There are quite a few chapters here that echo the other books. Why the repetition? Everybody connects to magick in a different way. If you get what you want from Damon's books, you might not need this book. But there are other powers on offer here, and a different way of getting where you want to be. The more powers you have at your disposal, the more likely you are to find magick that works for you.

You might find *this* is the book that you turn to in a crisis. Or it might be a book that fits into your life just at certain times. Everybody is different. What I like about this book, without bragging or boasting, is that it works directly with *your* will, connecting you to a specific energy of magick that enables change. It is different from anything else. It feels different, and the results have a different quality. I think you'll like it.

Also, this book contains a unique section on emergency magick, showing how to get magick working even when you feel desperate. Normally, a desperate lust for your result makes the magick fizzle out. Not here. That's pretty special.

All the magick in this book works. That's a mightily bold statement, but I'm sticking to it because it all works if you follow the instructions and put your heart into the magick. Take the hint! Put your *heart* into the magick. Easy to do, and a lot easier than not doing magick. A life without magick is too difficult, too ordinary. I think we can do better than that.

The Sigils of Creative Light

When you call on the power of a sigil, the transformation you connect with is the same power of alchemy that has worked through the ages for many others. These images are more than archetypes, more than symbols. They are a direct connection to ancient magick that has worked from centuries ago, right through to the modern-day. It has always worked, so it *can* always work.

This ritual process takes your desire, your decision, and your will, and amplifies them through the magickal code of a sigil, impressing your intent on the fabric of the universe. The universe responds by making reality match the vision of your magickal consciousness.

We have come to know the images in this book as Sigils of Creative Light. That sounds kind of New Age, but there's more to the name than meets the eye. In magick, every act is an act of creation. And creation never means making something from nothing. It means taking what is already there and changing it. Magick is always an act of alchemy, a moment of transformation. Magick is about *change*.

To make something new, you change what is already there. If you want more money, you don't create more money; you attract money that already exists. If you want more peace or balance, you transform your state of chaos and imbalance to one of stability. Whether you work in business, the arts, or a trade, you create by shifting and changing what already exists. To get a better life, you create by changing your reality to contain more of what you want. This is true creativity. That is why we call this magick Creative.

The word Light is used because there is no harm in causing change in accordance with your true desires. There is a lightness of touch to this magick. It can work powerfully, with great force, but the quality of the results feels somehow wholesome and in keeping with who you are, never leading you astray. Light is also a powerful symbol in magick. You may sense a light emanating from these sigils. Or you may not.

Doesn't matter. But light is the engine of magick. You are a wellspring of desire, and every desire you have is a force of pure white light that channels through you and into the sigil. You never need to visualize this for it to work. This just happens. But now you know why we call these Sigils of Creative Light. They cause change, and the energy that fuels that change is your desire.

Sigils of Power and Transformation was originally the title of just one section of a much, much larger magickal volume that has not been published. During the past year or so we decided that our planned book was far too long. So long that the heavy volumes might damage your bookshelf. We're splitting it all up, and I'm really proud to share this part with you. So here you are, with the Sigils of Creative Light offered to you as a source of Power and Transformation.

This is a safe system of magick, using the distinctive power of sigils, and the secrets that make the magick work - emotional energy and perspective shifting. The sigils do most of the work for you. All you need to do is perform the ritual, and allow your emotions and thoughts to shift ever so slightly as the ritual happens. This takes no massive effort, only a small act of will. If you can do this, you can wield magick of the highest order. If you've worked with other books by The Gallery of Magick, much of this is the Emotional Transmutation that you're familiar with, but some of it is not quite the same. You get a new way of working here, that triggers the magick. If you're completely new to magick, you'll pick up the skills in no time. Magick doesn't get much easier than this, but don't let the simplicity fool you into thinking it's trivial or slight. The title contains the word *Power* for a reason. When used correctly, you can make colossal changes, and that is power. The power to transform yourself, your circumstances, and your life.

When you've read all the instructions that follow you can, and should, look through the book to read about the sigils and their powers. It's perfectly safe to look at the sigils, and you may even find that some of them call you to work with them.

The Source of the Sigils

I've hunted down sigils of all shapes and sizes since I was a teenager, always looking for the best, the most authentic, ancient, and powerful images that could help me. But something that didn't occur to me for such a long time is that no matter how sacred, powerful or magickal a sigil might be, it was still something that a human being had drawn. That sounds so obvious. Of course, sigils are drawn by people. But in the occult community, sigils are treated with such reverence you'd think they were hand-drawn by an angel.

It could be true that some sigils were inspired by angels and described in visions by spirits. That's what many people claim. But it could also be that sigils were crafted by people in the *hope* that they would work, that they would contact higher power, and then they started to work, because of some mystical magick process that theorists love to waffle on about.

Bottom line, the sigils work, whoever drew them. But I'm pretty sure that a lot of sigils were not inspired by angels or any spirits. Some of them were just made up, and then they started to work because they were used in a magickal context, with an altered state of consciousness. If this sounds fanciful, a quick glance through occult history will show you that some of the most famous names in occultism went to great lengths to come up with sigil creation systems.

These systems might even be called something like the Science of Sigils, but it was still made up. These occultists just invented new ways to make up sigils. If there were no known sigil for a spirit, they'd make one up, using a complex formula to make it seem more real or valid, especially when they called it a magickal science. Which makes me wonder – were they *all* made up? Is every sigil a human invention, reaching out to connect with magick? It's more than possible.

This made me a bit angry and confused at first because it made the whole thing seem fraudulent. I wanted to believe that for each spirit there was one *genuine* sigil. One *right* sigil. Finding the *right* sigil is like having somebody's phone number or email address; get it right, and you make contact. Get it wrong, and nothing happens at all. That's how I saw things.

I should have known better because as my sigil collection grew, I saw that each sigil appeared in many versions and variations, and some were wildly different. Sigils were drawn by many hands, redrawn and altered (deliberately or through sloppy copying) changing to be unrecognizable over the centuries, but they still worked. What magick was preserved in these distorted images? This began to fascinate me.

As I got older (not much older, but a tiny bit wiser), I stopped obsessing about this too much, because I had to get on with my life. The sigils I used *worked*. It didn't matter that they were drawn by people. It didn't matter whether it was the oldest and most authentic sigil. All that mattered is that it worked. And then I dived into Chaos Magick, making my own sigils, and finding them almost as effective, and sometimes *more* effective than the 'real thing.' If some occultist could make up a sigil a few centuries ago, what was to stop me doing it now?

If sigils are used with faith and hope, magick starts to work, even if you've made it up. In theory, you could make up one hundred and eleven sigils for yourself. Yep, it could work. But you know what works better? A sigil that has been used this way for many decades, based on magick that is centuries old. That's what you get in this book. And then you don't need faith, hope, willpower, or years of power-building.

The sigils I share with you here are something else altogether. They are not an attempt to contact a spirit. It is *possible* these sigils feed on the power of angels and other benevolent forces, and if you're an expert you may even see scribblings in there that look like angelic names – possibly, a bit smudged and changed. But most of the imagery in the sigils is not clear. And it is my belief that what you're connecting to is the pure essence of magick that is scribed into these images. These versions were drawn recently, but their origins are somewhat older, based on images that are much, much older, meaning they've worked for many people, for a long time. This gives you power.

I believe that the creation of these sigils involved more than academic and historical study. I have come to believe that the sigils here were created during inspirational trance. It was a combination of extensive magickal knowledge, and deep trance, that led to their formation. The sigils were born of magick and based on ancient magick, and this gives them immense power. But what is the story behind this particular collection of images?

The Sigils of Creative Light originate from a private collection of materials that came into the hands of The Gallery of Magick some decades ago. Ever heard the word grimoire? It sounds like a book of authoritative magickal facts. We think of grimoires as collections of perfect, true, and accurate magickal ideas and images. Truth is, a grimoire is a personal collection of magickal ideas and thoughts, being a bit like a magickal journal. Some are a few pages long. Some are more like a treasure chest, with masses of confused material. Some are full of theory, some are filled with practical methods, and many are unclear, hurried records of experiments and ideas. They are more than magickal diaries, but they are never the whole truth. They are too personal for that. Generally, they are one person's private record of an exploration into magick. Sometimes, a handful of people contribute to a grimoire. There's a lot of junk, but the good ones contain important discoveries.

The private grimoire that we gained access to is undoubtedly a mix of the old and the new. The keeper of the grimoire was not the author of the sigils, given the way he writes about them in the accompanying text, but it appears he knew the person who created them. As such, they are not ancient. The accompanying text suggests that using an awareness of ancient sigils, and an inspirational trance, what you see in this book was created over the space of several years, between 1922 and 1928. But the imagery they are based on has probably been worked and reworked for centuries.

None of this matters if the sigils work, right? But I think it's important to know that the sigils were collected, tested and used by a reasonably large group of people, long before we got our grubby hands on them. They have been in secret circulation for some time. This matters because, when something works for many people, it is more likely to work again. I could make up a personal sigil tomorrow, and it might be very powerful. I could share it with you (or sell it to you!), and it could still be quite powerful. But only after a few *years* of shared use would it get powerful enough for me to say, 'Here we go, you can use this, and it definitely works.' That's why I'm so confident about the sigils in this book. They have been used successfully, repeatedly, and most importantly, they have been used on modern problems.

Some of those old occult texts I was talking about – they are full of cures for toothache, worms, bowel problems, dirty water, and indigestion. It makes the magick feel old-fashioned and irrelevant when it's easier to pop down to the dentist, or the pharmacy, to get your cure than to spend weeks chanting. But old magick can apply in the modern world. In some of our books, you can find magick that helps you to prevent computer hacking, but as you probably worked out, computer hacking really wasn't a problem a few centuries ago. But keeping secrets *was* a problem. It's the same essential problem. There are ways to adapt old ideas to new situations. The sigils in this book may be based on very old problems, but they have been wrought in a way that makes them hit the target of the problems you face today.

The big question is: *how do they work?* There are some rabid occultists who insist that all magick must work with spirits, or it's just not magick. I disagree. But if these sigils aren't connecting you to an angel, what's going on? It's my suspicion, my best guess, that when these specific sigils were created, they were based on *several sets* of more ancient images, and combined to reflect aspects of power held within those sigils. A cosmic mashup of magick. From the scribblings and notes that accompany the sigils, that's the best guess I have. The *combination* is what counts. This fits in with a lot of the theory that I believe. But what's far more important is that the sigils were then used in the context of a magickal structure that helped them to work.

And so they were used, and they worked and then that made them work more. What works in the past becomes stronger in the future. The images become embedded into the stream of creative light that powers magick. This is a long way from being scientific, I know, but from a life spent meddling with magick, and then thriving with magick, my belief is that these images are now a direct way to tap into the pure light of creation. You pour your will into them, and it's amplified into reality.

For you, this means that staring at the sigils connects you to every other success these sigils have brought. It means that with a minimal effort, you get where you want to be. Everybody who hears a song or reads a poem has a personal interpretation based on who they are. It's the same with a sigil. You are unique. The way that you connect to the magick will be unique, and the magick will respond to your specific needs.

What you're tapping into is the creative spirit of humanity itself - the best that we are when we succeed, overcome and achieve, perceive and advance. Often in magick, you can sense ancient spirits - something that feels familiar and strange and very 'other.' The same can happen with this sigil magick because you sense the ancient spirit of humanity, a fragment of humanity that strived to better itself through the supernatural and altered states of magick. This is a collective human spirit that has grown and evolved in the modern era. You connect with the essence of what it is to be a creative, spiritual, and successful person, and you connect to the very magick of our humanity.

Since the sigils came into our possession, they've been drawn and redrawn many times. As that happens, inconsistencies and changes creep in. The ones we use now don't look quite like the originals. But this is OK. There are many ways to say the same thing and be understood, many ways to draw a tree and still know that it's a tree. Have a look at this mess of scribbles.

Lots of different styles, but you know that every one of these squiggles is the letter A. It's the same with a sigil. It doesn't have to be exactly the same as an earlier copy. If it's close enough, it works. The next image is an early version of a sigil.

What follows is the final render that's used in this book:

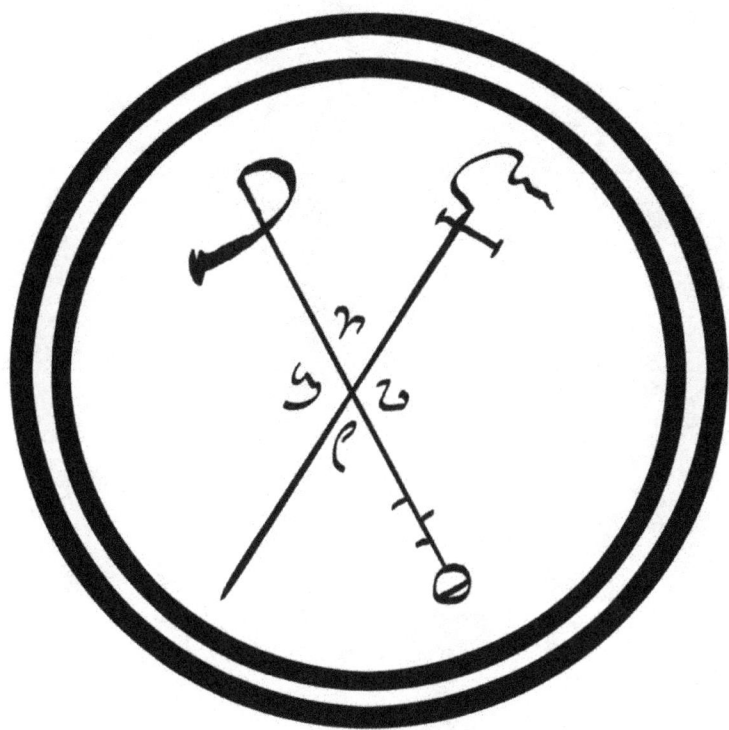

The early version is fairly different from my final sigil. Both work. What you get in this book works.

The two outer rings are based on experimentation more than tradition. We've found that this particular spacing of rings helps to draw the eye in, during the magickal ritual.

And that's all you need to know. The magick is ancient, it's modern, it's a mystery (and a fairly confused history), but it works.

How to Use the Sigils

You could summarize the ritual process as simply as this: you look at the sigil and think about what you want to change. That's all the instruction I had when I started out, *before* we deciphered the background materials. It wasn't clear whether you were meant to glance at the sigil in a candlelit room or stare at it for hours under a noonday desert sun. What we tried worked, but not as well as it works now.

Now we know more, and what comes next is a set of instructions that you should follow, step by step, word for word, nothing more and nothing less.

When you have chosen a sigil, you're going to need five or ten minutes to work the magick. Turn off your phone, go somewhere quiet and private, hide in a closet if you have to, but make sure you won't be disturbed. If you are disturbed, it jolts you with a moment of guilt and surprise that's just not ideal for magick. If everybody in your house knows that you do magick, fine, tell them you're going upstairs to perform a ritual, and they'll leave you alone. Whatever your circumstances, find a time and space where you will be undisturbed for ten minutes. Without this, it's difficult to obtain the calm and focus that's required.

You *can* do this magick sitting on a park bench, or while pretending to read in your armchair, or even while pretending to work in the office, if you are certain that you won't be disturbed. If you are disturbed slightly, by noises or distractions, that's no big deal – just carry on. But if somebody asks you the time, or to pass the salt, or shows you a video of a dancing cat, you've been pulled way too far out of the magick, so just stop, and start again sometime later in the day. No harm done, so long as you do it again later. But save yourself some time and make sure you won't be disturbed.

If this sounds difficult, have some sympathy for me when I was a teenager, trying to draw chalk circles on the driveway outside my house, in the dark, and then removing the evidence by morning. Be very glad you only need this book and don't have to go around drawing circles in cloudy moonlight. You can see why I try to keep magick simple.

You've found a time and a place. Now follow these steps:

Step 1. You want something. That's why you're doing magick. So whatever you want, that's your *desire*. Let your desire build. Feel the need.

Within desire, there is always lack and frustration. Feel this. Feel the desire, feel the yearning, feel what's missing. Might be huge, might be slight. Whatever it is, feel it. As you do this, you look through the sigil. You feel the desire for change, and as you look through the sigil, you let that desire build.

Yes, I said look *through* the sigil. This is easier than it sounds. Inside the double circle, there's lots of white space and the black lines. To look through the sigil, you gaze at the white space as though you are looking through the sigil to a white light beyond. It's as though the black has been painted on glass, in front of a brilliant white light. It might not be that spectacular – it might just be like looking at the white bit of the page, rather than the black bit. It still works. But you let your gaze rest on the white space, as though that's the white background you are trying to see. The sigil itself is just something in front of the white. Put simply, look at the white bit. Can't go wrong.

You can choose anywhere inside the double-circle, right near the center or off to the side. I prefer the center, but it really doesn't matter. But pick one spot, and try to keep your eyes there, rather than roaming around. Your eyes *will* move but guide them back. And more important than anything: what your eyes do *doesn't matter* half as much as your feeling of desire. Work on the feeling of desire more than your eyes.

The following diagram shows two places you could look at, but really, anywhere within the circle will work.

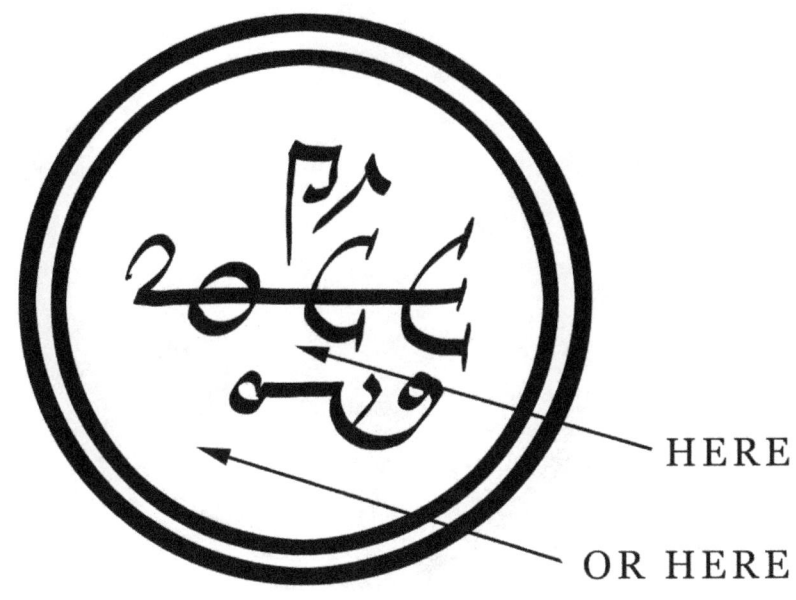

When you do this, you will not be able to keep your eyes still, and you are going to see the circle, the lines of the sigil, maybe even your hands and bits of your room, whatever. Doesn't matter. Look at the white, as though you are looking through, and that's going to be OK. This part of the process lets you see the sigil without focusing on it. The image sinks in. If you glance at it accidentally for a second, you won't do any harm.

Often, the sigil seems to distort during this phase. Distorts and wobbles and goes in and out of focus, and even vanishes. Or not. Whatever happens is OK. Just look through the sigil, and remember the desire. You *can* do two things at once, right? It's not that difficult. Let your desire build, and look through the sigil.

This is an artist's impression of how it might look, but it's just an impression. It might look more normal to you.

You don't need to do this for more than half a minute – even ten seconds might be enough if that's all you can manage. And that feeling of desire doesn't have to be heart-poundingly strong. Just feel *some* desire, look through, and that's it. If you don't have *any* desire, you don't really want this result enough. Feel what you feel, and then go straight to the next step.

Step 2. You make a decision that this is *not* how things are going to be. Staying in a state of desire is not acceptable. You choose to move to satisfaction. This is your decision.

Decision is not the same as hope or a wish or a desire. Decision is your intention to change the way things are.

You're not going to make things change by ordinary means, but by supernatural means. But the important thing is that you make a decision. Your decision is that reality will change so that your desire is satisfied.

Don't fuss about the details. It's like deciding you're going to get fit. You don't need to know where to buy running shoes or which gym to join. You just make a decision. Easy.

As you allow this feeling of decision to arise, move your gaze from the white background to the outer rings of the sigil. You can do this as soon as you start to make your decision, or if you prefer, wait until the feeling of decision really builds. This is a purely personal choice. The decision feeling might happen super-fast, or might warm up slowly.

Another artist's impression, showing how the rings dominate your vision now, but you can still see other stuff.

You can circle your eyes around, or try to see the rings of the circles at once in a single, steady gaze. You're bound to see the rest of the sigil, and all sorts of other things. Doesn't matter. Get your focus on the circle, and *feel* your decision. Things are going to change. Know it in this moment.

I can't tell you how important this decision is. Hope and yearning and longing are nothing compared to the power of decision. A decision made during a magick ritual - that makes things happen.

33

This part of the ritual might last only a moment or two. It can take longer if you're trying to build up a feeling, but usually, it just clicks that this *is* your decision, and that's it. If it's taken half a second and you haven't even glanced around the circles once, move on. If it takes longer, then pause and ask yourself if you really want this change? If you're not sure, repeat Step 1 until your desire is so strong that you can't help but make a decision.

One final reminder: you don't need to know how your decision will play out. If you decide to make your money go further, that's all you need to decide. You don't need to know what, when, how, or anything else. You're only making the decision that this is going to change.

Step 3. Turn your attention to the black lines within the sigil itself. You can scan your eyes over each detail, or just gaze loosely and take in the various shapes. You will see other things besides those lines, but keep your eyes mostly on the lines.

It might look like this:

Your will is not something that's forced out with effort but is a calm certainty. It is the absolute conviction that this is how the universe is meant to be. With your decision, you have acknowledged that the current situation is wrong. Now you need to pour your will into how things *should* be.

You scan your eyes over the shapes in the sigil and allow yourself to imagine how you would feel if your problem was solved. When a problem is solved, it's easy to miss it. Yep, that's right, we take normality for granted because it's just so... normal. Have you ever been so sick with flu that you've taken every cold and flu remedy known to humanity, and you're sucking lemons and chewing garlic and promising that you'll really appreciate life if you can only get better. But then you get better gradually, and you forget that you were ill and you don't even notice your relief. You got exactly what you wished for, but barely even noticed.

Sometimes, relief is more obvious. You're horribly in debt, and a kind old uncle gives you $10,000. You feel immediate relief and gratitude. What we're looking for in magick is the kind old uncle – the really obvious feeling of *wow, phew, that's better*.

Creating this emotion is easy. Imagine that your problem is solved. While you're in the ritual, at this point, you imagine that it's solved and see how you feel. Even if it's not a big problem, you'll feel some relief. When you think about it, the desire you have is a source of tension. Getting what you want relieves that tension. So feel the relief.

As an example, if you were using the first sigil in this book to Enhance Concentration, you might need better concentration for an upcoming exam. You're frustrated because after an hour of study you start drifting off and surfing the net and being lazy. It's annoying and frustrating and damaging your potential. It follows, quite naturally, that if somebody waved a magick wand and gave you instant Enhanced Concentration you'd feel relief. Well, that's all you do. Imagine you get your wish right now. Feel as though it's already happened. Notice how that feels. It's dead simple.

While this is going on, you keep looking at the black lines and shapes of the sigil, not staring, but looking and seeing the shapes, as you feel the gratitude and relief.

If you've read our other books, all that bit that I've described is the familiar 'emotional transmutation,' and it's one of the great keys to magick. In the other books it usually ends here, but in the next step, we take it a bit further. If you haven't read the other books, doesn't matter a bit, but don't move to Step 4 until you've really felt gratitude that the problem has already been solved. (You know it hasn't, not really, but just pretend, and feel *as though* it has.)

Step 4. Make your gaze soft, so that the sigil is barely in your awareness (but still in your field of vision). Your eyes rest on the sigil, but you're not staring, and you may not even focus. It's in front of you, but your focus is more on how you feel. If it helps, look through to the white again like you did in Step 1. It might look like this.

Imagine that it's many years from now, and you *remember* your problem being solved, and how *easily* it was solved. It seems easy and obvious, in hindsight, like the natural order of the universe. Things worked out easily. It seemed like a big problem, but it wasn't. 'Of course that all worked out,' you think. This might take you out of your comfort zone because you have to pretend or imagine, and that can feel weird or daft, but trust me that this is essential. Pretend it's ten or twenty years from now, and your current problem seems like a distant memory.

Why? Because this is how problems work out. A decade later, even the worst divorce, the most terrible bankruptcy, the scary diagnosis – you look back and go, 'That seemed like such a big deal, but I don't know why I was so uptight because it all worked out. Sure, it was rough for a while, but I'm so glad it all worked out.' Bring this feeling to magick and the future will reshape to give you that feeling in the future.

It's true that some problems remain in our lives, and never fade, so I can't honestly say that time makes *everything* seem easy or trivial. I look back with bitterness and anger at things that happened to me that I never managed to resolve, before the culprits skulked out of my life. But ignore those facets of your life. Overall, when you look back, the things that seemed like a big deal just aren't a big deal now.

If you don't believe me, think about your high school sweetheart. Are you still filled with heartbreak and longing, or do you just smile warmly? Remember how uptight you were about your exams, your first job interview, a date that seemed important, the plane flight you missed. There are a million moments that feel like tragedies at the time, but then they become amusing memories or anecdotes, and they make you see that problems *diffuse over time whether they are resolved or not*. Time is power.

'I don't have a good imagination!' I can hear you screaming it. I've learned many things about magick, and one is that ordinary people have imaginations that charge magick to the highest levels possible. You don't need to train your imagination in any special way. I also know that everybody thinks their imagination is hopeless. It isn't, so trust me and know that you've got what it takes to do this. I promised there'd be no need for amazing visualization and that promise holds true. This works even if your imagination is as weak as a newborn pony. We daydream all the time. We imagine being in the future all the time. All you're doing in this ritual is daydreaming more deliberately.

At some point in your life, you've probably imagined winning the lottery, meeting the perfect partner, sacking your boss, waving across the stadium at your adoring fans. Whether this was fantasy or intention makes no difference. You imagined how it would feel to be in that future. And when you fantasize like this, it feels natural and obvious and utterly real. If you tell somebody what you're fantasizing about, it sounds silly, and you feel stupid. But when you're daydreaming, it feels real and believable. That's all you do in this part of the ritual. Imagine that it's all worked out.

You might think this sounds the same as Step 3, the emotional transmutation, but there is a *big* difference, and the difference is time. In Step 3 you feel as though the problem is solved now, in the moment, and what a blessed relief that is. That's a near-future feeling. In this step, by projecting into the far future, ten years or more, you diminish the power of the problem.

I absolutely love this part of the magick, because it works so well. You don't have to know where you'll be in ten years, or picture yourself in a rocking chair or anything like that. All you do is pretend it's at least a decade from now and you're looking back, lightly, at what once appeared to be a problem, and remembering how easily the chaos was restored to order.

You might not have noticed this, but positive fantasies almost always have an element of certainty and a calm backward glance. *I got a high-paying job and ahhhh that feels so good because I remember when poverty seemed real to me.* Or *Ahhhh it's so lovely to have married Sarah, because I was so lonely, and fell in love with her so hard.* Or, *Ahhhh, it's so lovely to be single again after that hellish marriage.* It's not just relief you're feeling, but that order has been restored, things are as they're meant to be, and your life is back on track.

If you have trouble comprehending this, think of something that once seemed impossible, but that has worked out for you. If you've got a steady job, and it once seemed totally and absolutely impossible to find work, you will remember that illusory crisis with a sort of old, wise warmth, because you now know there was nothing to worry about at all. You must have a thousand examples from your own life. If not, your life really is terrible. And I don't believe that for one second.

That's quite a long description for Step 4, but this part of the ritual is over quickly. It happens as quickly as you can pretend to be in the future, and think and feel how easily that old problem was solved.

Another reminder: you don't need the answers now. You imagine the feeling, not the details. So if you're using the sigil to Make Noisy Neighbors Quiet, you don't need to know what will make them quiet. Are they evicted? Do they suddenly spend more time at the library? It matters not one bit. It's not your job to think about the details, only the overall feeling. If you force your own details in, you limit the power of the magick. Give the magick freedom to find a way, and it will find a way. If you imagine one way, your way, and insist on it – it probably won't work. In this example, you just remember how that noisy neighbor problem seemed so bad, but *ahhhh*, it worked out all of a sudden, and you got the peace you wanted and wasn't your home lovely and quiet after that. And that's all! Don't go into the details.

You close your eyes, and the ritual is over. Close the book. The whole thing takes just a few minutes. You perform the ritual once a day, at any time of day, for three consecutive days. And you're done.

Sigils in Practice

When I was at school, my chemistry teacher would explain something abstract, and I'd sit there praying for him to give me a real-world example. Eventually, he would, and *then* I understood. I'm a bit better at abstract thought now, but I love examples. So here's one.

You want to stop procrastinating. It's been a bad habit for a long time. It's only a couple of hours a day, but it all adds up. You don't want to lie on your death bed thinking about the 22,000 hours (that's three and a half years of waking life) that you wasted in excruciating procrastination. You want to stop procrastinating and get on with things. Pretty straightforward desire. You need to stop procrastinating. That's your desire.

You get comfy and start the ritual. No great ceremony required. You might want to dim the lights, set up candles and music, or you can just sit in the back seat of the car and hope nobody notices. Make it as normal or dramatic as you like.

You look through the sigil to the white beyond, and your desire builds. If the desire doesn't feel strong, think about how the frustration affects you. You're losing your life. It's ticking away. Every time you procrastinate you feel rotten and useless, and you hate how much time you've wasted. Dwelling on this negative stuff can really make you feel the desire. So feel it, see the white, and let your desire for change build. You want things to be different. You want to stop procrastinating.

How specific you make this is up to you. Do you want to stop procrastinating about everything, including the laundry, paying bills, weeding the garden - or is it just that you want to spend more time learning to play the ukulele? It's your choice but work with the desire you genuinely and authentically have, not the desire you think you ought to have.

In just a few seconds your desire is all fired up, and as you look at the white you might see the sigil wobbling and distorting, and you have to remind yourself to breathe and blink. But the desire is there, so you move to Step 2.

You look at the rings around the edge of the sigil, and as you let them into your vision you make a decision that you've had enough, this is it, things are going to change right now. You do not believe you are a procrastinator and you will not be one. The way things are now is in no way acceptable, and you choose to move from this feeling of desire for change, to satisfaction. Somehow (doesn't matter how) your procrastination habit is going to be obliterated. That is your firm and final decision.

You're not making an inflated promise to yourself, or a New Year's resolution type statement. You're recognizing that this is not how your life is meant to be, and you are deciding that you will change this reality with magick. *That* is your decision.

It only takes a moment, but you feel the decision strongly, so you get straight to Step 3. You scan your eyes over the shapes in the sigil and imagine that you no longer procrastinate. You let the relief flood through you. You feel grateful that the problem has gone away. If it helps, imagine yourself in a situation where you're getting on with things. Or you might need to say words inside your head, like, 'It feels so good to have stopped procrastinating. I'm so grateful I got past that.' Experiment. If you can just get the pure emotion of relief and gratitude, that's great. And you scan your eyes over the lines of the sigil all through this bit.

No need to linger in this state, so you let your focus soften. You imagine that it's many years from now, and you *remember* that time when you stopped procrastinating. It seemed like such a big deal, but you stopped so easily and wasn't that a relief. That's how things were *meant* to be. You let the feeling stay with you for a moment or two, then close the book, or switch it off if you're using the eBook, and that's it. Get back to normal by doing something normal – eating, reading, walking, peeling potatoes… What you don't do is sit there wondering how the magick is going to work. I think of this as like taking a shower. You get in the shower in the morning, and no matter how great it feels, you get out and then forget about it. No big effort, because it's no big deal. It's just something you do. Same with magick. Move along, please.

It's easy to imagine how this example applies to the rest of the book. You're feeling sick and achy – you know your desire, you know what decision you need to make, and it's very easy to imagine being healthy – no problem.

But is everything that simple? What if you want to Uncover Secret Thoughts? It seems so abstract. But it's not. You have a desire – to know the secret thoughts of somebody that affects you. You start the ritual, feel that desire, then *decide* that you will know these thoughts, then you feel grateful and relieved that magick has brought you this knowledge (even though it hasn't yet), and then you imagine looking back at this time, and you think, 'Remember when those thoughts were secret, and then I found them out. It all worked out so easily.' Or your version of that. Some people don't think in words but in pure thought and concept. Others think in pictures. Most people think in a mix of these all jumbled up. Whatever way you think is going to be OK.

For any sigil, if you think you want to use it, then there's an obvious desire that needs to be satisfied. The rest follows from there, and I don't need to spell it out. You know what you want.

The Flow of Magick

When you come to perform your first ritual, don't ask for a crazily unrealistic result. If you ask for a huge lottery win, or to be loved by everybody you meet, or to pass exams without learning and revising, or to become famous overnight, you're going to be disappointed. That doesn't mean magick is rubbish. It works well if you make a genuine request that's just out of reach. No point in doing magick for things that are already within reach. No point in doing magick for things that are utterly impossible. Go for things that are fairly out of reach now, things that would surprise and amaze you if you got them, but that still feel right for your life.

If you've been working at fame for twenty years, and you're almost there, then yeah, you can ask for fame overnight, because magick can push you that tiny bit further to get you into the limelight. But if you're starting out on the path to fame, you will use magick to take the small steps that everybody takes at this stage. The advantage *you* have is that more things will go right for you. But don't kid yourself that you can ask for the moon. Not all in one go. And fame is a really bad example because fame doesn't look that much fun to me. But my point is that whatever you want, whether it's a steady job, a spiritual revelation, a new direction or a breakthrough in your career, reach for something that seems only-just-impossible rather than a complete and utter fantasy. Do that ten times, and you get where you want to be much faster than if you do a ritual to get there all at once. I think we've said this in every book, so if you've read them all, you can wake up now.

And this isn't meant to sound patronizing or to minimize the power of magick, but you wouldn't believe some of the messages we get. 'Can I levitate?' is all too frequent. This book and everything I've stuffed into it is about working with a heartfelt desire, rather than a trivial or unrealistic wish.

Magick works, and it can work stunning wonders that will make you weak at the knees. But when you're getting into magick, it works best when you take small steps. Try to get rich overnight, and you're just kidding yourself. Some magick does work overnight. You *might* attract cash out of the blue overnight. Lots of magick works instantly. But take it easy. Don't be too demanding. If you do some rituals for huge results and get nothing, you might turn into one of those haters that sends us death threats. You don't want to be one of those people.

Take your time. It's been a few years since we started sharing magick and there are loads of stories of overnight wonders and things going right in an instant, but the best stories are when we hear that somebody has chipped away, working on the big things, the small things, the underlying problems, the spiritual fascinations, and after a year or two they look back and barely recognize who they used to be. Do that!

And – I'll keep this short, even though it's essential – if there's *anything* you can do to help the magick, you *must* do it. If you're trying to raise money, don't hope the magick will do it all. Go out and raise money. Sometimes there's nothing you can do. If you've done a ritual for money to appear out of the blue, then it appears, or it doesn't. Fine. Do nothing. But if you're asking magick to contribute to your efforts, you need to put in some effort too. Imagine you're standing in a crowd and you want everybody to run to the hills. If you shout, 'Run to the hills,' and stand where you are, eating a donut, nobody will move. If you run like crazy, looking back over your shoulder as though there's something chasing you, and shout, 'Run to the hills,' you'll get the whole crowd running. Magick is a bit like like that. Works best when you do your bit. So run to the hills.

Now I'm going to guess your top six questions:

What if I can't do the ritual on three consecutive days? Wait until you can. Or be half-hearted and break it up over a few days, but don't expect it to work as well.

What if I want to do more than one ritual at once? You can. You can do five in a day, or more. But imagine this. You've broken your leg, and so you get fat and unfit, and all your tendons and joints are stiff. How do you get back to full health? You wait for your leg to heal, for the bones to knit, and then you start hopping about, walking, jogging, stretching and building your way back to the life you had before you snapped your leg in that skiing accident. If you go jogging, or even stretching, while you've still got the cast on your leg, things will not go well. The bones will stay floppy, and nothing will heal.

OK, it's an extreme example, but lots of people approach magick this way. I want to get rich, so I'll just get rich right now and not worry about my debts and poor health and crappy relationship. Getting rich is *really lovely*, but does it have to be the first thing you do? Sort out some of the problems that bring you down, and you bring ease into your life, and then everything works more easily.

If you want to do one hundred and eleven rituals at once, you won't explode, but I don't think your magick will be exceedingly impressive. Find out what *needs* to change, find out what you *want* to change. Work on a small need and a minor want. Build from there. Slow and steady. Oh, magick works fast – so fast you'll wonder why I warned you. But a slither of patience and self-control might work better than an ambush of rituals.

What if I want to repeat the ritual? If you feel that way, it might be because you're being impatient. Results come at the most appropriate time. Might be instantly, might be gradual, might be weeks away. Don't repeat unless things really change and you get a strong instinct to do the magick again. If you're repeating out of fear that it didn't work, or that you did it wrong, well, there's nothing to stop you, but it might muddy the water. Try to do it right the first time. And you do the ritual for three days, so you're probably going to get it right somewhere in there.

What happens if I start to get results before the three days are over? Good question. You do a ritual to improve the mood of those around you, and it works that afternoon. And then the next morning you kind of don't want to do the ritual again, because everybody seems lovely and calm, and you don't want to generate the desire for change out of nowhere. If you feel that the desire is fully satisfied, stop doing the ritual. If, a few days later, it all goes rubbish again, then do another three-day ritual. Or, if the situation improves a bit, then keep going for three days, but modify the ritual based on the current circumstances. So when you get to desire, you desire things to be better than they are now. Don't go back to the feeling you started with on day one. If nothing changes during the three days, that's perfectly OK - just repeat the ritual the same way every day.

Can I use this with other magick? You can use this alongside any other form of magick, but you don't need to. People love mixing their magick up. That's up to you. But what you have in this book is enough to get results. You don't need to learn anything else. If you want to experiment by mixing different styles, experiment away. You might find the sigils add potency to something else you're doing, and that's not going to bother me. But if you're happy with what's in this book, then it's all you need.

Can I use this magick on somebody else? Some of the rituals already work on other people; the inspiration rituals, for example, and the ritual to ease people out of your life. What about the rest? Yes, you can. Imagine you want to help your sister to ease chronic pain. You find the sigil, and you think about *your* desire for her to heal. You feel *your* decision, *your* relief, and gratitude, and you look back at everything from *your* point of view. You might ask her permission, or you might not. That's none of my business. But don't hurl ritual results at people based on guesswork. Be certain you're sending a change that's wanted, otherwise it won't have any effect.

Emergency Magick

The whole point of the ritual process you use with these sigils is to reset the universe, as you see it. Your personal universe feels awry, and you restore order the way you want it to be, with magick, using desire, decision, and will. Most of the time it works the way you want it to, so long as you don't ask for ridiculous leaps of change. You're lighting a fire, not setting off a nuke.

It's interesting, though, that when you need magick the most, it can let you down. Don't worry; there is a solution. But when there's a crisis, when you feel desperate, and when you really want magick to work, that's when it can let you down. Desperation can deflate and whither your bold magickal efforts and make you feel pretty stupid for having done a ritual. But there is a way to get magick to work, even when you're feeling desperate for a result. That's pretty unique, and that's what this chapter is about.

When you need an urgent result, you might use magick to solve the problem, but have you ever heard of Lust for Result? If you've read anything about magick, you'll know that lusting after your result stops it from happening. You do your ritual for money, and you supposedly have to stop wanting the money, or the money doesn't show up. You do a ritual to end bad luck, but if you're obsessed with fear about the magick working or failing, the magick fails. Your bad luck gets worse. That's the contradiction of Lust for Result. It sounds like a complete pain, but there's a lot of mental and spiritual growth to be found in magick because you learn to overcome your Lust for Result. It seems like a bad thing but is often a good thing. But, let's be honest here. It can really be difficult to let go of desire when your need is strong. And if magick is going to help, it should help you when there's a crisis.

After everything we've said so far, in all our books, the shocking truth about magick is that it *can* work even when you are desperate for a result, when you're hoping and yearning, when you are slavering and lusting for a result. No, we've not been lying to you, but there are a few tweaks and modifications and mental tricks you need to juggle to get emergency magick to work.

Bear with me for a (long) paragraph while I go over some old ground. It's important. Trust me! Desperate need for the result is OK. What you need to avoid is the desperate need for a *magickal* result. There's a difference. Let's imagine that you want $200 to pay the rent, otherwise the landlord's throwing your sofa out the window. You've got no obvious way to get $200 without robbing somebody or asking your sister-in-law for a loan, and neither option is advisable. So you do a magick ritual. Does the money show up? The cold, hard, ugly truth is that if you can somehow forget about the money turning up, it's a lot more likely to turn up. But it's hard to forget about the money. If you can't forget about the money, then forget about the magick. You are relying on the magick, but pretend you're not. Pretend the magick never happened. Be careful, though. If you *dismiss* the magick, by going, 'Well that was a load of crap, so I don't think it will work,' you've just taken the batteries out of your magick machine. What you need to do is more subtle and cunning. You act as though you completely believe in the magick, but you couldn't care less whether it works. The key words here are 'as though'. You're still burning with desire for the $200, but you act *as though* the magick is real, but you're completely cool and relaxed and don't care whether or not it works. It might sound tricky, but it's not much to ask. A bit of mental playfulness and you get magick to work! You still care about the $200, course you do, but you don't care whether the magick works. There's a *big* difference. If you can't see the difference then I politely suggest that you ponder, meditate or do whatever you need to do to see the difference. Stay focused on *what you want* and not on the magick. Then when you get the result, *remember* the magick and love the magick and feel joy in the magick. That's just as important. If you can, do the magick this way. OK, that was a long paragraph. You've probably heard it all before. So what's new?

Trust, faith, belief, and all that stuff sounds just right for magick, but what happens if you feel desperate, frustrated, or even angry? Anger is the emotion that bubbles up when you feel that a situation is wrong and you're powerless to do anything about it. That's the opposite of the feeling you get with effective magick. Magick gives you power. So mostly, usually, I'd say that you should use magick to imagine that you get what you want and there is no need for anger. But let's take a closer look at anger. There are always clues in the contradictions of magick.

Anger is a fiery, red, dangerous, and mean emotion, and we should breathe it all out in a meditation of peace. Or should we? Is it possible that anger is a deep reaction to our sense of our place in the world? Anger could be sending a message about what needs to change. Anger could be the very energy that guides magick. Not always, but when you're desperate, anger can be a guide and an energy.

When you desperately want a result, you can feel pretty frustrated before you even start the magick, and you get worked up with doubt and anger before you even start. We often warn that magick amplifies your emotions, so the danger is that an angry person will just get angrier. We always tell people to let the anger fade before doing magick. Not everybody listens.

Damon Brand used to get angry messages from people that were like, 'Hey, I'm really poor, and I expected to get rich in ten minutes, and I paid MONEY for your book, but I did the magick three days ago, and nothing showed up, so you are a criminal for cashing in on people like me and getting rich, and I'm going to curse you, and I hope your children die.'

If that sounds like an exaggeration, trust me when I say that I'm actually toning it down quite a lot.

But the way Damon put it was that no matter how much *we* love the magick, no matter how *we* value the knowledge and no matter how cheaply we give it away for and think it's all *so* wonderful, we should have sympathy and empathy for people who are angry, because people *are* desperate, often living in desperate times and situations and magick is a last, best hope for freedom. If only people could direct the anger as a potent and pure energy, into the magick, these emergency situations could be solved.

For most people, magick works quickly and easily and - woo-hoo - we can all celebrate. For the desperate, magick can create more desperation, because you feel like, if this doesn't work, nothing will and the universe is so damned disappointing. I know how that feels. I have been desperate and frantic, foaming at the mouth for a result, poor and lonely in the early days, and I was furious at magick when it didn't work. Furious at everything and everyone. I may seem like a mild-mannered reporter now, but it wasn't always like that.

When I set out to explore magick, I was sometimes furious because I didn't have *enough* magick. It was very hard to come by, even if you went all the way to Watkins Books in London. There just wasn't much available, not in the way of practical magick. Lots of theory and charts, but not much you could actually *do*. Today, you can get just about anything you need for the price of a few mangoes, and you can download it seconds after making your decision – an hour later you can be *doing magick*. I'm not the first person to notice that this makes people take it all for granted. Try not to take it for granted! You don't need to grovel before magick, but if you treat it like a cheap trick, it might ignore you.

I'm just blowing a lot of hot air unless I can solve this problem of emergency magick. So here goes. Frustration, anger, and all those other emotions are your inner truth screaming out at you that something has to change. Those emotions not only send you a message; they give you a source of power.

For many years I've collected stories of emergency magick; magick that worked when it shouldn't have, when there was fear, anger, desperation, and despair. If you've read any of our angel books, you'll know that we instruct you to speak to the angels with polite authority, because this is a thousand times more effective than begging. Usually. In my years of anecdote-gathering, I heard many stories of angels responding to desperate pleas and helping people who begged. Magick is not as straightforward as it appears, and finding consistency in all this was elusive. So elusive that I never actually found the answer until I decoded some of the materials from the grimoire mentioned earlier. What I came to see is that when you truly beg and plead it's because you believe this is absolutely how it *should* be – there's no doubt, only conviction and sincerity. And then I understood all the stories I'd gathered or been told. Why was one person ignored by an angel, when another begged and was heard? It was down to the sincerity, to the inner conviction. This is not about belief, but about what you see as being right for you.

It's like you're saying, 'I insist that things be this way, because the way the world is right now, is absolutely utterly wrong.' If you go into magick with that level of fierce, fiery conviction, it doesn't matter whether you beg or command – the conviction carries your message. This means that if you're feeling angry and frustrated, there is a way to channel your anger, frustration, fury, and desperation, especially with sigil magick.

You've already seen the answer in the instructions I gave earlier. The essence of this magick is desire (born of frustration), decision (which is almost like a moment of anger at how things are now), and will (which is your utter conviction that things should be different). As you've probably worked out for yourself, there is a place for anger, but it's not meant to be there all the way through the ritual. If you're going to use anger, let it fire up your desire and trigger your decision. After that, use the methods described to let the anger dissipate. That's how you encode your conviction into the magickal process.

This means that there's a place for your anger and frustration within the ritual. But don't take it home with you. Don't bring it back out of the ritual. If you're stuck, desperate, furious or despairing, then you can use that emotion to kick the magick into gear. A pleasant side-effect is that you should find your anger and frustration ease up, and you generally get more chilled out about the problem. This is a good thing.

Let's be absolutely clear: you do not need anger and desperation to get this to work. If you can, use the instructions as set out in their most basic form, with your simple, strong desire being all you need. Remember that long paragraph from earlier – that's the standard way of doing this magick. Only resort to anger if you're overwhelmed with anger.

To summarize, if you feel anger, desperation, or frustration, during Step 1, when feeling your desire, let your rage and fury rise. Honestly open up to the anger and desperation, and even if you feel more anger and frustration than pure desire, that's OK, just feel it. When you come to Step 2, make your decision, and you can do so with rage. In the same way you might shout, 'Stop!' to somebody who's spray-painting your car, you can feel the emotion of, 'Stop! No More!' in Step 2. Your decision can be born of rage and desperation. But as soon as your decision is made, you head to relief.

In Step 3 you experience relief, but remember this comes out of a certainty that your decision is right. So although your anger and frustration should fade now, you can let them give you the energy to feel that relief. Have you ever come in from the cold and had a lovely hot mug of drinking chocolate? So much nicer than if you're offered one on a summer's day. It's the contrast that gives you the relief. But make sure you get to the relief. Feel that, *ahhhh, thank god my rage and frustration can fade away now because my decision is made*. Remember to feel as though you already have your wish. It's been granted. No need to be angry anymore. And then you move to Step 4, as normal, and that should be easy.

Emergency magick is not the craftiest form of magick. A cunning person plans ahead, using magick to stimulate and guide an exciting life. But accidents happen, and sometimes you will feel desperate and angry. If so, use this method. If not, keep it simple. Whatever version you use, don't sit around waiting for results. A watched kettle never boils. It does, actually. I've tried. But magick is more subtle than a kettle. When your ritual is over, ignore the magick you've performed as much as you can, and when you least expect it, it boils!

The Sigils and Their Powers

In the following fifteen sections, you'll find all one hundred and eleven sigils, with mini-descriptions of their powers and how you might use them. I've kept the descriptions short and sweet for a few reasons, and not because I want to avoid more typing – but because too much prattle can do more harm than good. If there's a sigil to Encourage Deep Sleep, you don't need me to go on about the benefits of deep sleep. It's obvious. The descriptions offer clarity when the sigil's power may be a bit more ambiguous.

I could write pages and pages about each sigil, but less is definitely more. It's important that you feel your way into these sigils. I'll say no more than that, except that I've given enough information for you to sense whether a sigil might be worth trying. More detail would only confuse your experience, and experience counts more than expectation. If you get a sneaky suspicion that a sigil *might* work for you, don't worry and fret about whether or not you're right - just try it out. The magick only takes minutes, so why not give it a go? Trust your intuition and work with the sigils that feel right for you.

THE MAGICK OF THE MIND

For the first set of sigils, let's start off with the mind because if you sort this out, everything else is easier. Concentration is undervalued, so use the concentration ritual whenever and wherever it applies.

If you have an interest in dreams, there are two rituals that help, but if not, what about a look at the ritual to recover a sense of joy.

You can take some of the mental clutter away and feel joyous again, which supports your life, your relationships, and your magickal work. This is a short part of the book, and one that seems less than vital, almost throwaway, but I bet you come back to this bit again and again.

In this section, you will find sigils to Enhance Your Concentration, Increase Dream Recall, Understand the Messages in Dreams, Experience a Lucid Dream, and Recover a Sense of Joy.

Enhance Your Concentration

Use this sigil any time you need better concentration. Might be an exam, might be a whole year at university, might just be an important day at work. You can use it for short bursts of concentration, or for long-term focus. Your desire will define exactly how long it works for. If it's long-term, there's nothing to stop you topping up for special events; specific things you need to learn, or exams. There are no limits on how often you can use it, but one long-term working lasts well.

Enhance Your Concentration

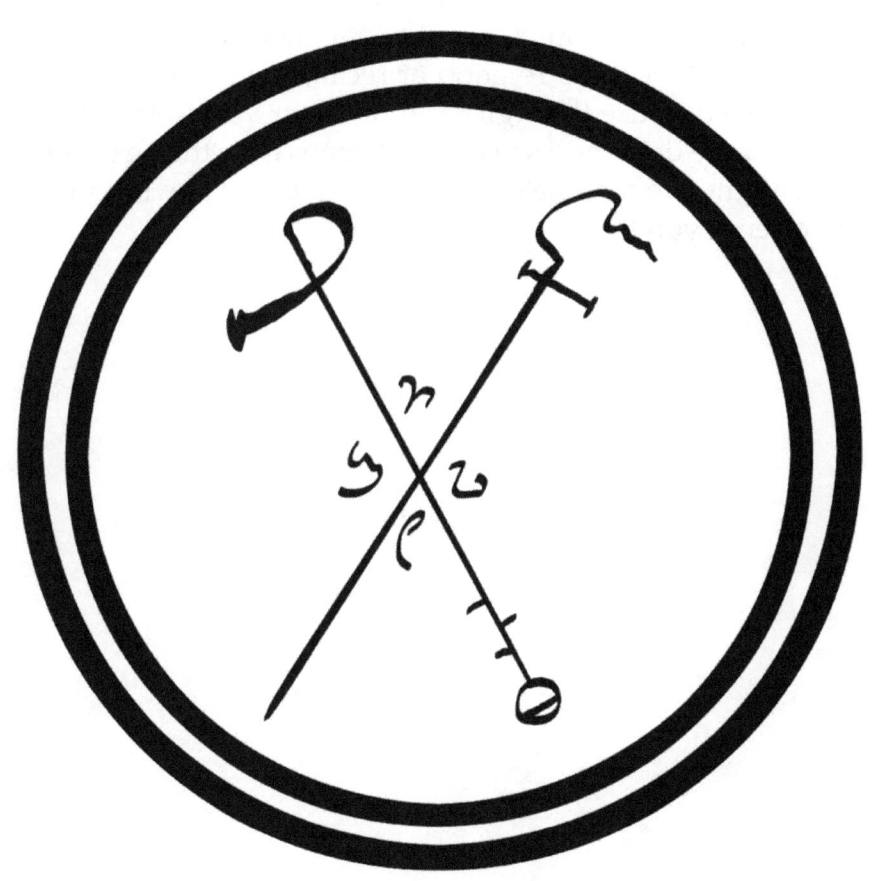

Increase Dream Recall

Everybody knows that if you write down your dreams, you remember them better. But this sigil can add an extra potency to your dream recall. Some people say it works best just before bed, but that's up to you. You might get good results using it in the morning. Once you're good at recalling your dreams, you may not need to use the sigil for months or years. At the start, use it for three days, and see what happens over the next month or so, and then repeat the complete ritual every few months, or more often if you like.

Increase Dream Recall

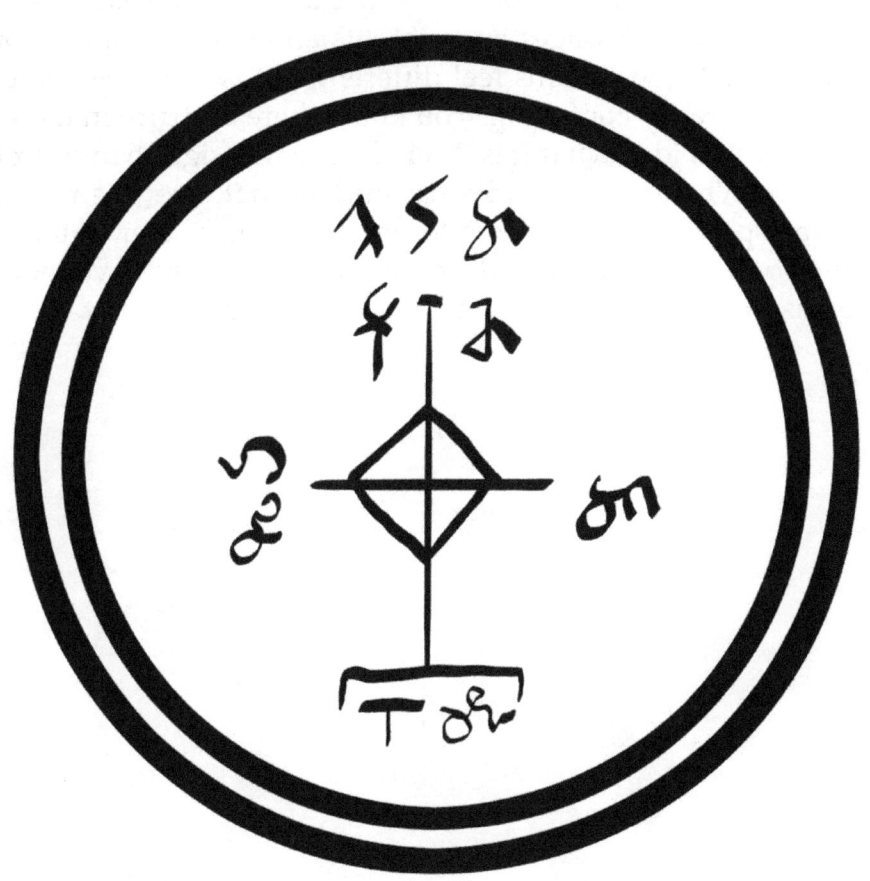

Understand the Messages in Dreams

I still believe that *most* dream content is just brain-waste, being discarded as important mental sorting dribbles through the brain's cogs and gears. But *some* dreams are special. Some dreams contain messages and insights and truths that cannot be ignored. These dreams feel different, but when they come, they can be really confusing. You know there's a truth in there, but you've no idea what it is. You can use this sigil to interpret a dream. When you've had a dream like that, use this ritual. The interpretation may come to you at a much later date, or while you're doing the ritual. Sometimes you might have more dreams that elaborate on the original sensation.

Understand the Messages in Dreams

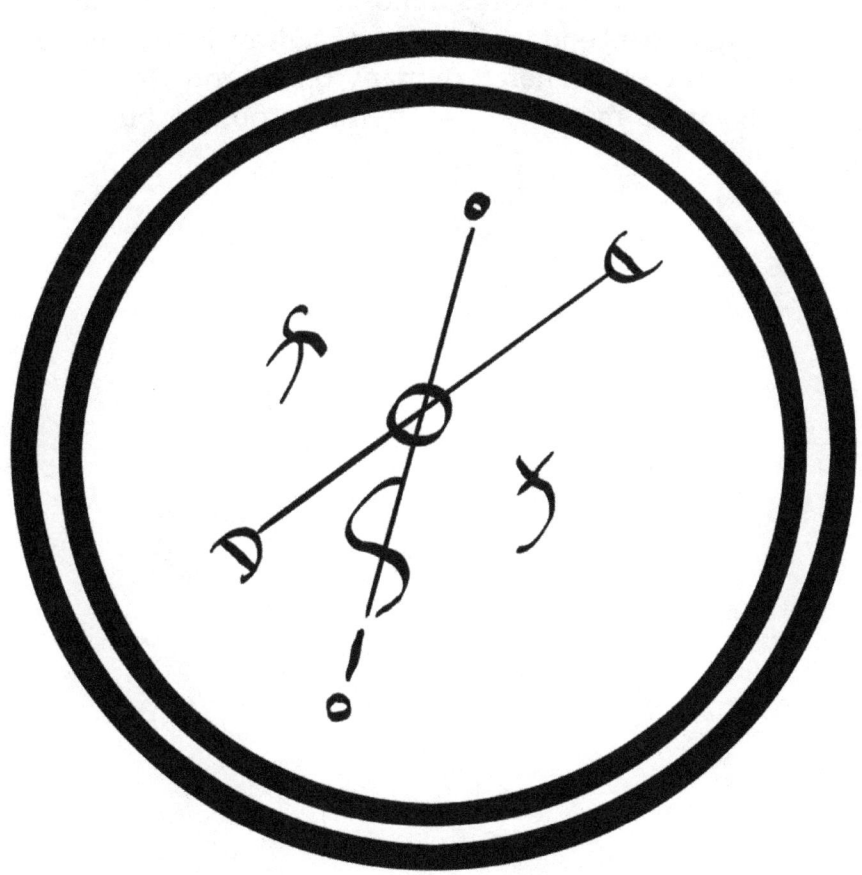

Experience a Lucid Dream

I've found the best way to have a lucid dream is to wake up about three hours before normal, drink a glass of water, and then go back to sleep. Works almost every time for me – the sleep's so light that I end up dreaming brightly. If I use this sigil, it works even better. There are many books and websites out there with similar methods. Use anything you like, but use this sigil as well.

Experience a Lucid Dream

Recover a Sense of Joy

Life isn't meant to be fun all the time. There's a huge range of vital emotions, and life should be a fragrant and heady mix of these varied feelings and experiences. Watching a sunset while feeling melancholy is underrated! But this sigil can help to boost your enthusiasm for life when your enthusiasm gets dulled. If you find that you're not exactly depressed, but life's a bit repetitive and boring, this sigil helps you to see what is already good in your life. This might sound like a really boring sigil because you don't want to be happy with what you've got; you want to *change* your life! Yeah, I get that – the whole book is about change, I promise. But changing your life from a joyless state is not as easy as changing it from a state of enthusiasm. If you're able to appreciate what you have and where you are, it's easier to get to somewhere new than if you're weighed down by resentment. Recovering your joy, appreciating what you have now – this is a powerful place to work from.

Recover a Sense of Joy

INSPIRING OTHERS

There's magick out there for influencing people to do and think what you want, but this part of the book is more about offering inspiration. You might do this to make your life better, or out of generosity. If the people around you are moody and bringing you down, it's your right to inspire a better mood in them. Everybody benefits. Compassion and warmth are often locked away beneath cold and grumpy habits. Using magick to get people to lighten up is high magick. There's magick here to get more understanding, love, trust, and to help others achieve change and transformation.

In this section, you will find sigils to Improve the Mood of Loved Ones, Improve the Mood of Those Around You, Uncover Warmth in Others, Encourage Compassion, Encourage Understanding, Encourage Love, Encourage Trust, and Encourage Change and Transformation.

Improve the Mood of Loved Ones

You love your family and friends, but they can really bring you down. This magick can be used when the mood is just starting to slip, or even when there's been entrenched angst for many years. It won't change habits and preconceptions and all the other stuff that makes friends and family so infuriating, but it will lighten their mood, and that can be enough.

Improve the Mood of Loved Ones

Improve the Mood of Those Around You

This sigil is similar to the last one but works on people who are not really loved ones – people you work with, people you meet or travel with. If you're with people for a day, a year, or ongoing, this ritual can urge those around you to cheer up a bit. They remain the same people, so you're not going to get perfection, but a sour mood can be sweetened.

Improve the Mood of Those Around You

Uncover the Warmth in Others

This sigil can uncover the warmth when somebody is frosty with you. Useful at work when there's somebody who believes that being professional means being like a robot. Useful at home when problems and anxiety make people hide their warmth, or just forget it through habit. It can be used in relationships, friendships, and whatever warmth is there can come out. A very pleasant sigil.

Uncover the Warmth in Others

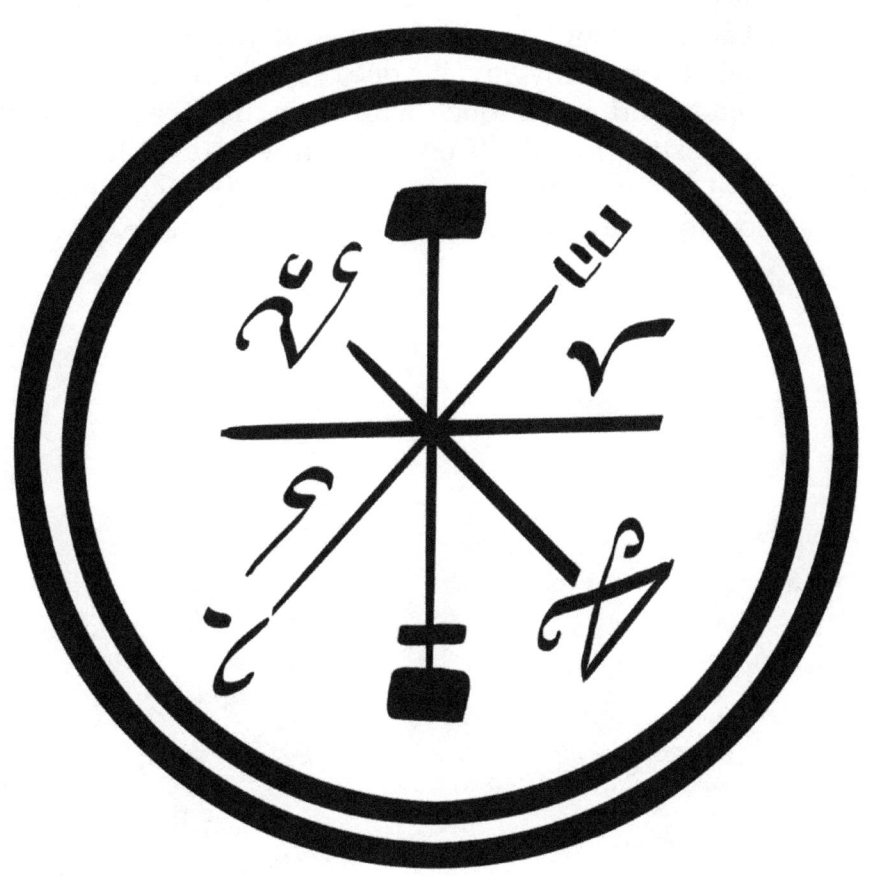

Encourage Compassion

If somebody has no compassion, use this sigil to bring it out. Have you ever seen a family arguing at a funeral? I think it happens because there are so many mixed emotions. It also happens because people are fighting over the will, and who pays for the flowers. Anyway, it's one of those times when you wish people would get in touch with their compassion, rather than all the nasty grime that's on the surface. It doesn't have to be a funeral… Any time you need somebody to have more compassion for you, your situation, or anything else, use this sigil.

Encourage Compassion

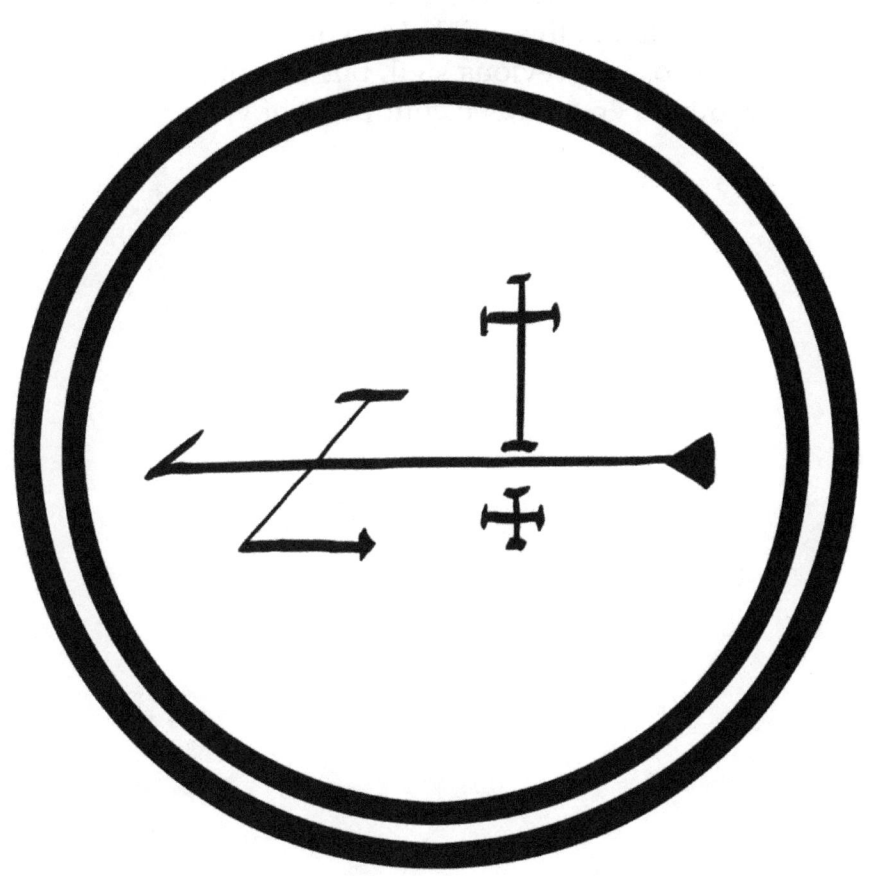

Encourage Understanding

I've found this sigil works to make people less critical because they manage to have a bit of empathy and understand things from your point of view. If you need somebody to understand you or your situation, this will help to open up their mind and heart. Similar to the previous sigil, but this one's more about getting the other person to see your point of view.

Encourage Understanding

Encourage Love

This one does what it says and encourages love, so use your imagination. It can help to encourage non-romantic love from a friend or relative. It will encourage spicier love when romance is already simmering. This magick will only *encourage* love, and won't create it from scratch, so there needs to be something there for the magick to work with. It won't make a stranger fall in love with you. But if somebody loves you, deep down, or has the potential to feel that way, this will encourage the love to be felt, experienced, and expressed.

Encourage Love

Encourage Trust

A lack of trust takes many forms. Your partner might not trust your driving, or for you to look after the kids, or for you to do the taxes – and this lack of trust can make you feel unloved. Your workers might not trust your motives. Your boss might think you can only take on so much responsibility. Or there might be a downright suspicion that you're a criminal, or that you're up to no good, or having an affair. Wherever you need trust, this sigil can encourage the other person to let go of their fears and doubts about you.

Encourage Trust

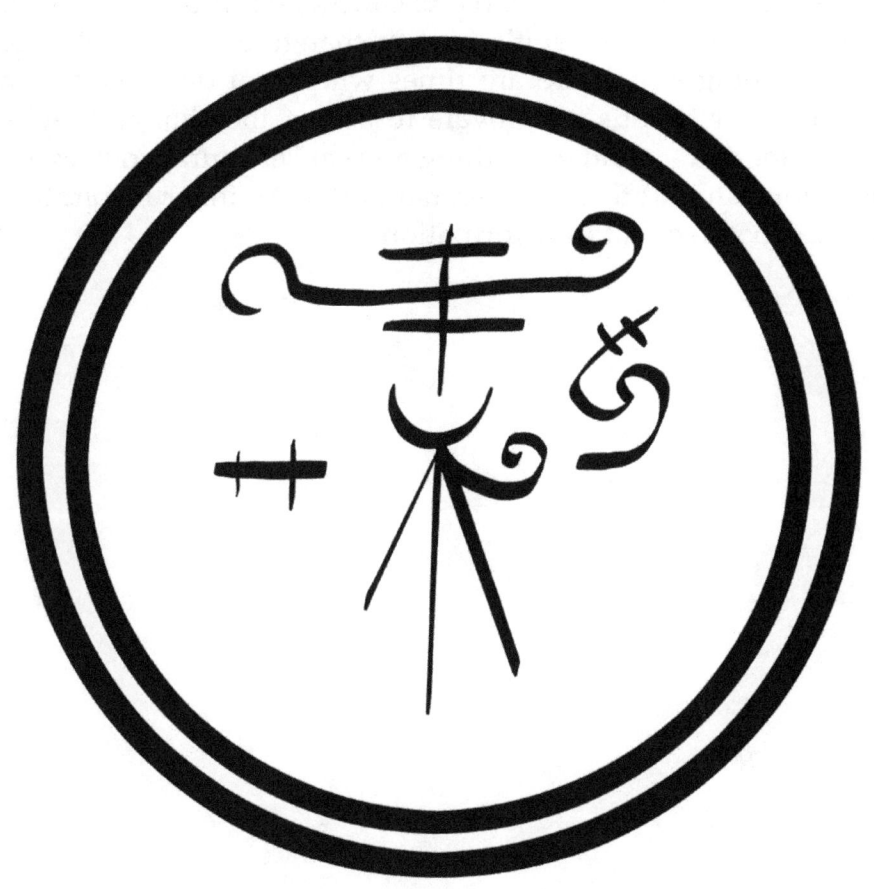

Encourage Change and Transformation

Have you ever watched a loved one teetering on the brink of change? It can be so frustrating to watch the worry and fear prevent them taking that leap into college, stand-up comedy, or starting a band. Whether it's a career change, a personal change or something else, there are times when you dearly want to inspire your friends and lovers to accept the change they're drawn to. You've said everything you can, encouraged in every way you can, but this sigil can help offer the inner inspiration it takes to make that transformation.

Encourage Change and Transformation

EXTENDED PERCEPTION

Psychic powers are about as predictable as the weather. There are patterns, but always surprises and disappointments. But the sigils in this section can unearth psychic abilities even if you think you haven't got that ability. It's easy to try, so why not see what happens?

In this section, you will find sigils to Uncover Secret Thoughts, Sense the Near Future, Sense the Far Future, Recover a Lost Object, and Connect Psychically with Another.

Uncover Secret Thoughts

If you think it's immoral to look into somebody else's secret thoughts, I get that. But this sigil is aimed at those times when you really want to know what somebody is thinking because you believe it will help. You know, when somebody looks upset or confused, and you can tell they're holding something back. You might be worried they're being bullied, or that they've fallen out of love with you, or that something else even worse is going on. Often, it's really nothing, but if the person isn't willing to open up yet, it can be a wise and wonderful thing to sense what it is they are going through. You're not spying and invading, but establishing communication in a highly unusual way. If you really want to know what somebody is thinking, it should be somebody who's close to you, and the ritual should be performed with both your best interests at heart. You might get an immediate sense of the truth. It might occur during the next conversation. Sometimes the other person finally blurts out what they're really thinking. I've found this sigil to be very effective, and a lot faster than other methods.

Uncover Secret Thoughts

Sense the Near Future

This won't give you a general idea of what's coming up in your life, but if there's something that affects you, that you're concerned about, where you really want to know the details, and no matter how many times you get your Tarot cards out you don't get the reading you want, this sigil can be what you need. There are many ways for you to get a sense of the future, from dreams to flashes of certainty. With this sigil, it can be anything, but the most common is a gradual sense of knowing that comes over you during a few days. It works for things that are going to happen within the next two or three weeks.

Sense the Near Future

Sense the Far Future

When you need to get a vibe about the far future – things that will happen within the next year, but more than a few weeks from now – use this sigil. You might want to know how your business will develop, or where you're heading in relationships. If you have a genuine desire, rather than a whimsical interest, this sigil will reward you. The knowledge comes to you over a few days, as a sort of knowing, a sensation of what the future holds. If you have a specific question, such as, 'Is it going to be a good idea to move to that new company?' (or whatever your question may be), then you will get a strong feeling that tells you what you need to know. But you should know you're not getting an answer from a higher power. All you're sensing is a possible future, and you still get to decide your fate.

Sense the Far Future

Recover a Lost Object

This one's as simple as it sounds. Often, it works in minutes, and you don't need the full three days. It will only work if the object is findable. Sounds obvious, but it works if the thing you've lost is somehow within reach. If it's been moved to another country, ground to dust or fallen to the bottom of a lake, nothing will happen. Sorry, but that's how it is. If there's any way it *can* be found, this works so well it can feel a bit weird. Things can reappear, or be returned to you, seemingly from nowhere. Sometimes you get a strong hunch, and that guides you back to the lost object.

Recover a Lost Object

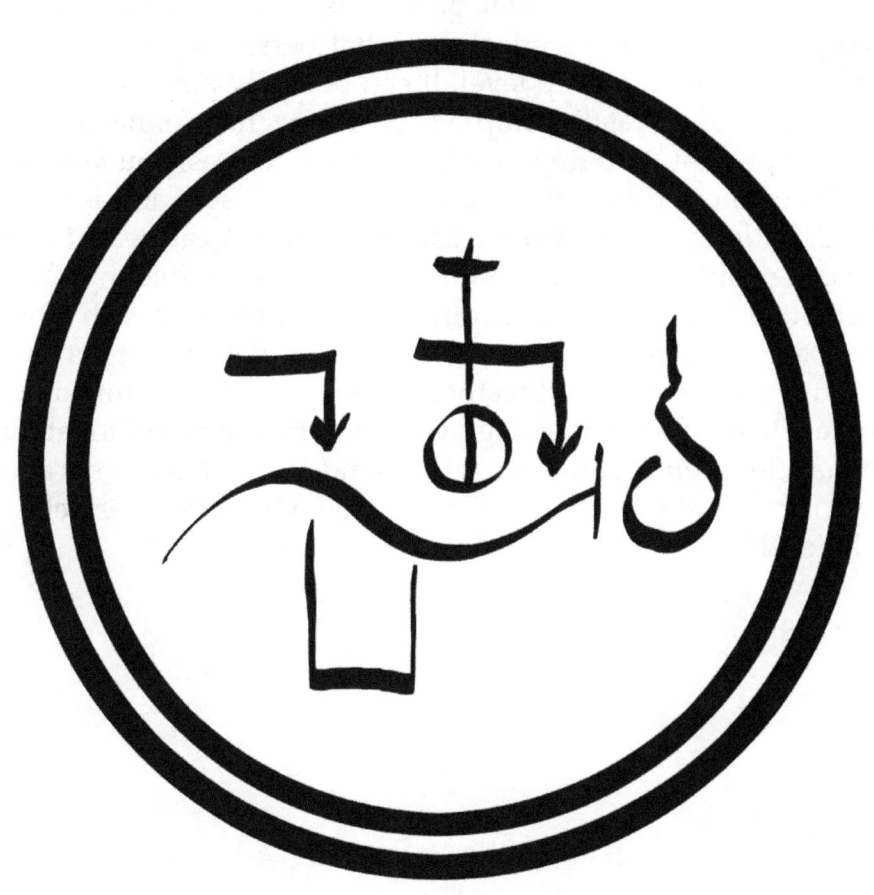

Connect Psychically with Another

If you want a psychic connection with somebody, using this sigil can make it happen. It works best if you both do the ritual. It can also work if the other person has no idea what you're doing, but will only be effective if that person trusts you and welcomes you on a deep level. It can be really powerful at the beginning of a relationship when a psychic connection is already present. You finish each other's sentences; you feel like you're connected on a really amazing level. Use it at this early stage, so long as you trust each other, and it can lead to an amazing connection. No, you're not going to be able to talk to each other like you're on the phone, but the sense of each other can be quite strong, and sometimes complete thoughts and feelings will be passed directly between you. The results often come when you're not trying, when you're dozing off together in the afternoon. It can work with friends, as well as lovers and partners, but the bond is easier to forge when it's a very close relationship.

Connect Psychically with Another

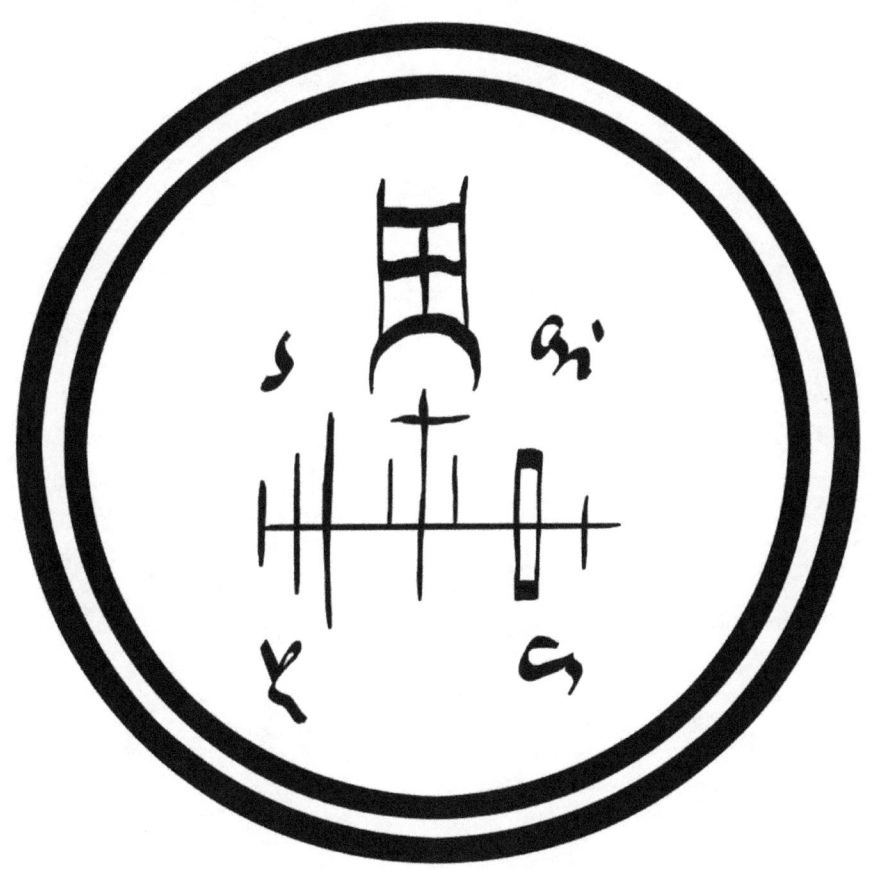

FORTUNE

This section is all about luck, or what *appears* to be luck. But luck is a cheap word, so I called it 'fortune' instead. These rituals help nudge the odds in your favor.

In this section, you will find sigils to Obtain a Fair Legal Decision, Be Seen in a Good Light, Thrive in Competition, Make a Good Decision, and Be Given a Chance.

Obtain a Fair Legal Decision

If you want a fair legal decision, luck shouldn't be an issue, right? But it often is, because other people get lucky, have better lawyers, or whatever else. Get this ritual done in the days that lead up to the decision, and it will make sure your case is dealt with fairly.

Obtain a Fair Legal Decision

Be Seen in a Good Light

It shouldn't take good fortune to be seen in a good light, but sometimes it does. This sigil works for a few days at most, so its best used at a critical time – family gatherings, meetings, that sort of thing. It makes people see past your faults and notice all that's good about you.

Be Seen in a Good Light

Thrive in Competition

This won't help you win a lottery or game of chance but will help in any form of competition where your effort counts. That might be a competition for the best landscape painting or the 100-meter sprint. Perform the ritual in the days leading up to big events, such as a race. Or if it's a long-term project, where you have to work for months to create your competition entry (as with the landscape painting example), use it when you start out, when you get stuck, and when you know the judges are about to see your work.

Thrive in Competition

Make a Good Decision

A good decision should be based on knowledge, self-awareness, intuition, and many other facets of your sparkling character - not good fortune. Should be. But when you look at your life, how many times do you think, 'Oh wow, I was so lucky I made that decision.' If you've got a big decision coming up – which job to take, which house to buy, that sort of thing – use this ritual and let the decision become clear to you in the following days. Trust your gut.

Make a Good Decision

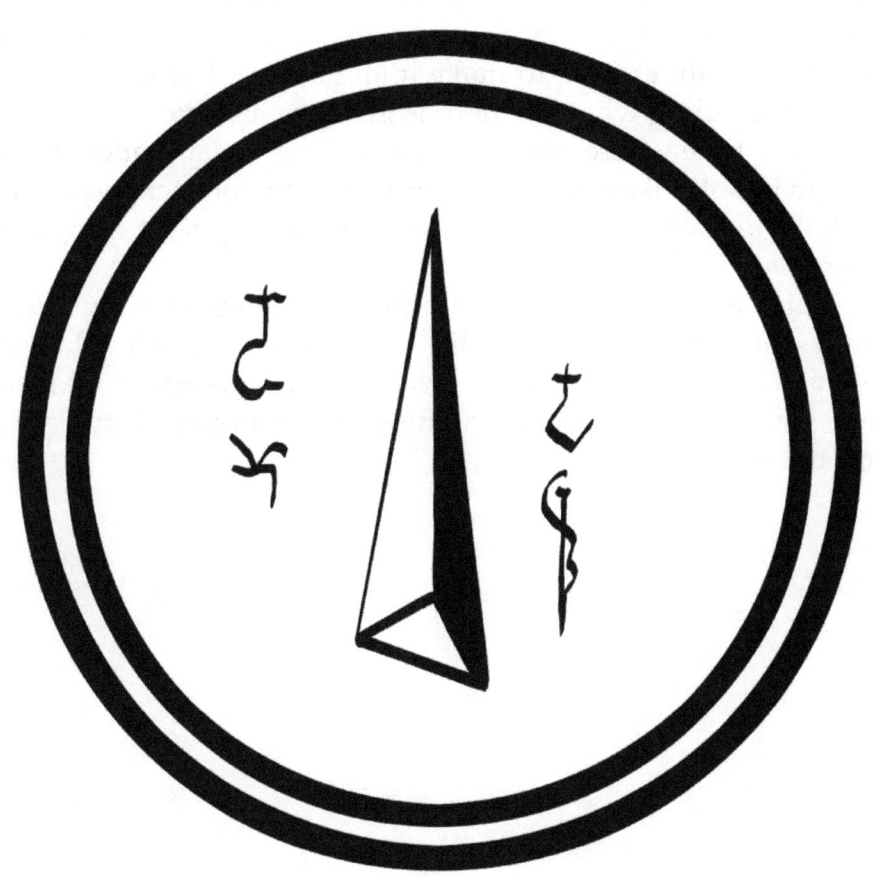

Be Given a Chance

I love that moment in movies when the young apprentice is being rejected by the great master, and it looks like all is lost, but the apprentice begs, 'Just give me a chance.' Sometimes the master gives in straight away. Sometimes it takes an unfortunate street fight to make it all happen. But it's a really satisfying feeling when the hero is given a chance.

Any time where you just want to be given a chance, even though it looks like you're the wrong person, too inexperienced or that the stars aren't aligned, use this sigil to shift things in your favor.

This is a mighty sigil. I'm light-hearted about it, but, you know, this one can be a real life-changer. Use it only when it really matters that somebody gives you an opportunity. Make sure you're ready to make the most of the opportunity *before* you use the sigil.

Be Given a Chance

LOVE AND FRIENDSHIP

There is nothing here to seduce, persuade, or cajole love into existence, but there is plenty of lovely magick for getting good friends, helping love to thrive and solving some of the problems that crop up in relationships.

In this section, you will find sigils to Attract Worthy Friendship, Recover Lost Love, Attract Romance, Discover the Feelings of One Your Care For, End a Relationship Peacefully, Become the Centre of Attention, Attract Love Over Long Distance, Maintain Love Over Long Distance, Embrace Your Loyalty, and Renew Passion.

Attract Worthy Friendship

This sigil has been used by me, and several people I know, when moving to a new area. It's very difficult to make new friends these days. Maybe it always has been, but my work led to me moving around a lot, and it was always a pain. I found the same thing when travelling. I like to make friends when I travel, and this sigil has really helped speed things up – even though those friendships rarely last, they are worthy and memorable. It's also a great sigil in your general life. If you've got a huge list of Facebook friends, but very few people that you actually trust, that you really connect with, use this sigil. It's a strange one, because it works in many different ways, with chance meetings and coincidences helping friendships to spring up out of nowhere.

Attract Worthy Friendship

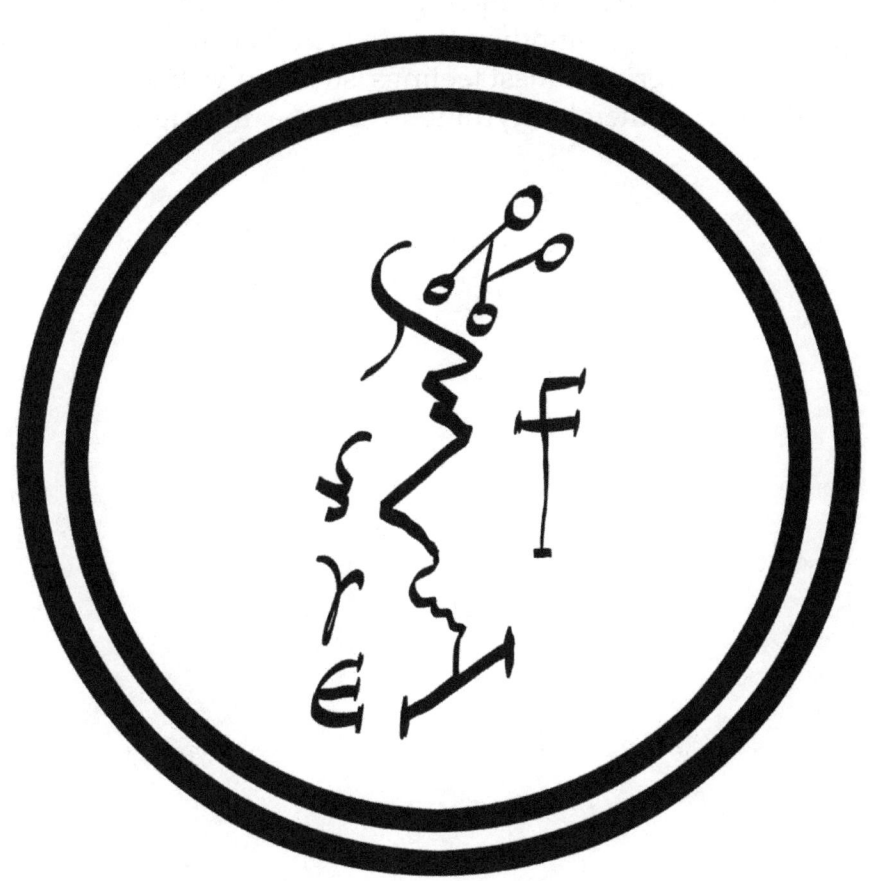

Recover Lost Love

What a wonderful sigil. You've lost your love, and now you want to get things going again. OK, that's the good news. It can work, and it can heal wounds, get everybody to forgive and forget and give you another chance. The bad news is that it works by uncovering honest feelings, so if you've truly lost that love, it's gone. If there's anything to salvage, this sigil *will* help.

Recover Lost Love

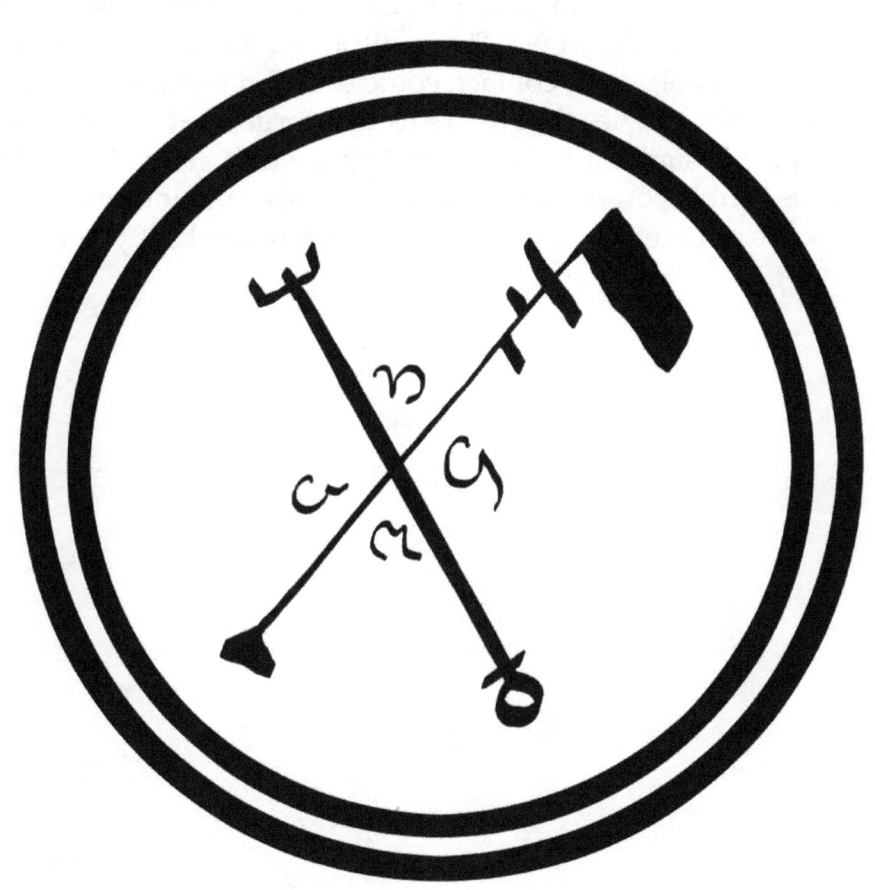

Attract Romance

This is not the sort of sigil you use before a date, in the hope of getting things to go well. It's not used to make somebody specific fall in love with you. You use this one when you want to meet somebody new. Those little moments that make romance possible – eye contact, coincidental meetings – all that stuff from the movies that happens to be true, that's what you get with this sigil. Sit at home, and you won't get calls out of the blue. But if you're out in the world, this can work in a few hours. It's not always so fast, so give it a few weeks if you have to.

Attract Romance

Discover the Feelings of One You Care For

You've met somebody and fallen in love. Great. But do you reveal your feelings, or might that risk ruining a good friendship or a happy working relationship? If you want to know how the other person feels before making a move, use this sigil. You might get a jolt of emotion, one way or the other, that gives you the answer. If not, if you feel nothing, notice how the other person interacts with you over the next few days. It should be revealing. A word of warning. Sometimes, you get a very clear signal that, yes, this is it, romance is happening. So you announce your love and the other person says, 'No, sorry, I just want to be friends.' If that happens, it might be because the magick has put you ahead of the game. You have inside knowledge and you spoke before the other person knew their feelings. So you still need to be cautious. A date might be wiser than a declaration of love. And it's also worth remembering that people don't always want to act on their feelings. If that's the case, be patient. Don't be a stalker, saying, 'The magick told me that you love me.' I don't think that would ever work. But being serious for a moment, this is actually a beautifully reassuring sigil. Sometimes what you get is profound disappointment, but at least you know the truth, which is better than not knowing.

Discover the Feelings of One You Care For

End a Relationship Peacefully

This sigil won't do the hard work for you. At some point, you still have to end the relationship by telling your partner that it's over. What the sigil can do is give you the strength to do this with honesty and dignity, while giving your partner strength to see the positives that can come out of this. Even the happiest of breakups aren't all that happy, but this really does help lessen the drama.

End a Relationship Peacefully

Become the Center of Attention

Before using this sigil, ask yourself if you really feel up to being the main event at the upcoming party. If so, great. This isn't going to give you charisma that lasts for months, but it can make you shine at one particular event, or even for a day or two. If you know a special event is coming up, and you want to stand out, use this sigil. Remember, though, that if you want peace or quiet time with one person, it might be more difficult than usual. As with all magick, you have to put your own effort in. But you don't have to dance on the tables to get noticed. A small effort from you should make you the center of attention.

Become the Center of Attention

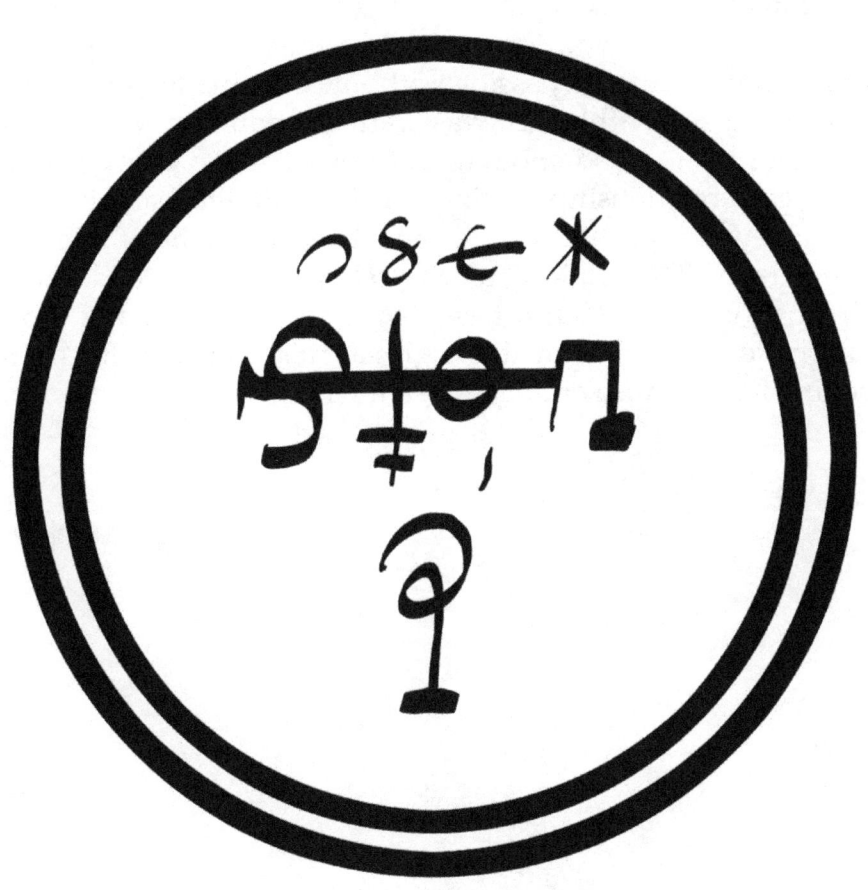

Attract Love Over Long Distance

This sigil was under my nose before I even knew about the internet. I'm not very old, but old enough for that. And I thought, yeah, it makes sense that in the olden days you'd have written to the one you love, who lived far away, hoping you could fan the flames of passion without being in the same place. Maybe that's why this sigil was crafted. I don't know, because my history isn't good enough. But now, with so many people starting up relationships online, this is a sigil that can help. It's not one that's been tested as much as the others, because members of The Gallery of Magick have never had much personal need of it. But it has been used by others, and those who have worked with this sigil say it's effective. If you're looking for romance online, give it a whirl.

Attract Love Over Long Distance

Maintain Love Over Long Distance

Long-distance relationships have never been easy. Are they easier now, with Skype and email and messages? I'm not so sure. I think it's always difficult, but often necessary. If you are apart from your loved one, for a couple of weeks, or half a year, work with this sigil to find the strength to get through. It can make the connection between the two of you stay so vital that it doesn't feel like an endurance test.

Maintain Love Over Long Distance

Embrace Your Loyalty

An interesting sigil, this. If you're tempted to stray from your lover, but don't want to, this can help you to remain loyal. You have to look at yourself pretty closely. Are you tempted to stray because it's actually time to end this relationship, or because you've met somebody you love more or is this just a fickle temptation? If you know you want to remain loyal, this helps refocus your heart on the person you are with.

Embrace Your Loyalty

Renew Passion

If your relationship has lost its passion, if you're taking each other for granted, this sigil can brighten this part of your life. You can use it alone, or with your partner.

Renew Passion

BREAKTHROUGH MAGICK

Some of the most important changes we make are the small, tiny, gradual ones that slowly shift us to who we are. But every once in a while there's a breakthrough, a big change, a total shift in who you are and how you live. These breakthroughs are an essential part of life.

In this section, you will find sigils to Open the Road to New Discoveries, Discover Creative Talents, Improve Creative Inspiration, Welcome Intuition, and Expand Available Time.

Open the Road to New Opportunities

Road Opening is an ancient form of magick in which you call on spirits, or the universe, to show you another way. If you feel the way is blocked, this is how you open the road. This sigil, although it doesn't call on spirits, helps to remove the obstacles that prevent you from seeing a new way forward. If you feel jaded, stuck, dull, bored or that you really need to change your life, but have absolutely no idea what might make you happy, use this sigil. Answers might come very slowly, or, you know, something might catch your eye and make you go, 'Yes, that's it.' This is very powerful magick when your need is real.

Open the Road to New Opportunities

Discover Creative Talents

If you have an urge to be creative, but don't know whether you should learn piano or take up poetry, this sigil can give you guidance. If you have no idea what you might do, or if you're trying to decide what's best, use this sigil to find out where your talents lie.

Weirdly, this can also work by helping you give up some creative work. You're taking singing lessons, and learning to dance, and those circus skills are really coming along, but hey, which should you focus on? This helps you realize where you're going to shine and what you're going to enjoy the most.

Discover Creative Talents

Improve Creative Inspiration

Writers, artists, musicians – need I say any more? You're stuck with a blank page, a boring portrait, or the same three chords. If you need inspiration for any art form, this sigil can break the block.

Improve Creative Inspiration

Welcome Intuition

Without a good sense of intuition, you make a lot of mistakes, and you struggle to hear the messages of magick. This sigil can help you welcome intuition into your life, or improve it if you're already quite intuitive.

Welcome Intuition

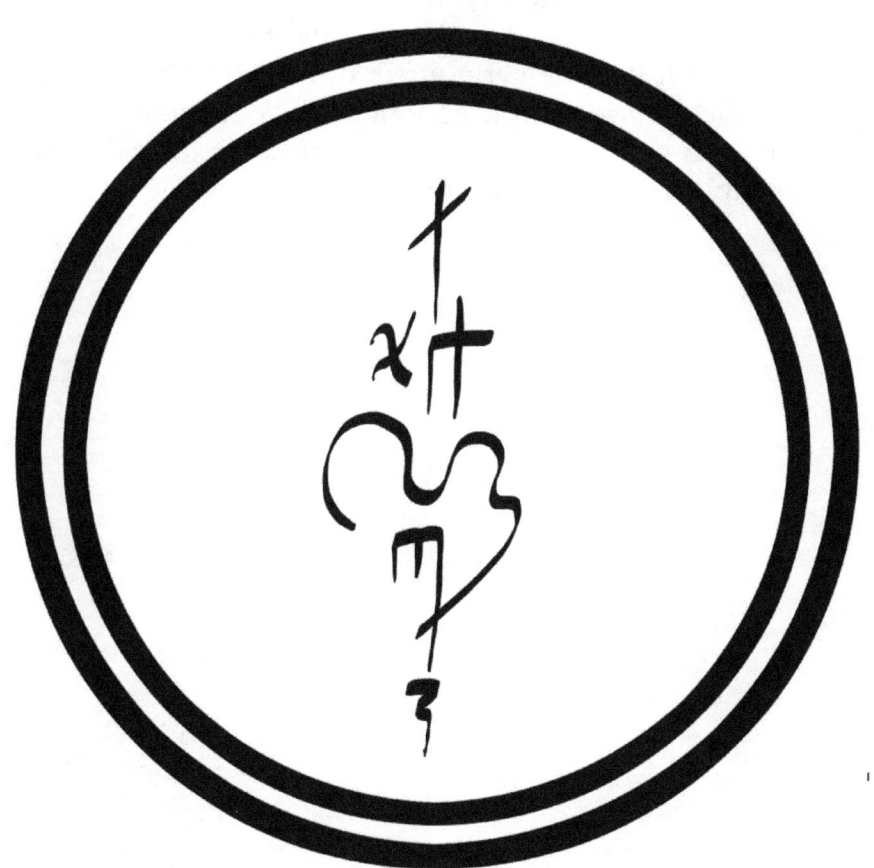

Expand Available Time

The ability to expand time is found in many magickal systems, and nearly every version I've tried is effective. So this sigil isn't unique, but it does work. If you've got a deadline, or just feel that you're so busy you don't even have time to water your plants, this sigil has the eerie effect of helping you get more done, with less effort, and it no longer feels like you're racing the clock. You can use it for a specific task, or to make more time available in your general life.

Expand Available Time

SPIRITUAL MAGICK

Spirituality means many things to many people, so I can't predict how this magick will work for you, or even whether you'll find it interesting. But whatever your beliefs, these sigils can stir something very real and vital. It's a peculiar experience, to use magick to attain spiritual growth, but it's one that can be surprisingly pleasant and rewarding.

In this section, you will find sigils to Sense the Spiritual, Discover Your Spiritual Path, Discover Your Material Path, Find Wisdom in Problems, and Discover Your True Passion.

Sense the Spiritual

If you feel that life is mechanical, meaningless, and devoid of mystery, this sigil can help connect you to the huge mysteries and emotions that you've hidden away. I could write so much more, but I encourage you to work with this sigil if you ever feel you're disconnected from meaning, purpose, and a sense of divine wonder.

Sense the Spiritual

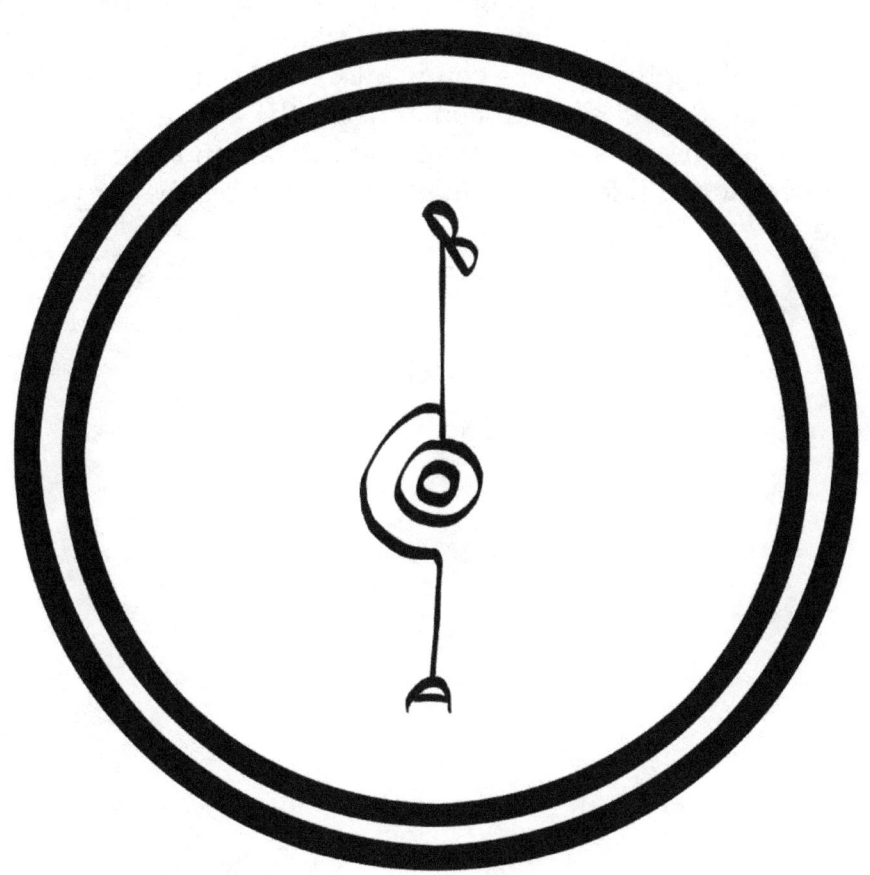

Discover Your Spiritual Path

You might be wondering, 'What is a spiritual path?' and answering that would spoil the fun. I couldn't answer it for you anyway. So what is this sigil for? I can only say that if the words, 'Discover Your Spiritual Path' trigger something within you, something that makes you want to find out, then use this sigil. Your desire should come from the sense that your spiritual journey has only brought you so far, and you want to discover more. I'll leave it at that, and let the rest be for you to discover.

Discover Your Spiritual Path

Discover Your Material Path

The first few Gallery of Magick books, all written by Damon Brand, were about money, power, sex, and all those material things that made some occultists wrinkle their noses in spiritual disgust. But something that's essential to the magick that we share is the idea that we don't transcend the material world, but learn to thrive in it. When the material world rules you – with fear of poverty and loss – you are in a weaker place, spiritually than when you are able to flow *with* the material world. You might never want to be rich, and that's great, but you may find there is a material path that you could take, and that in doing so you will obtain more spiritual growth than you have ever suspected. If you want to see where you could go in the material world, use this sigil, and expect the answers to come in the weeks and months that follow.

Discover Your Material Path

Find Wisdom in Problems

Magick is about changing things, taking control, and having power over your reality. Yep, that's the idea. But life is never perfect, and even the greatest occultist will never be free of accidents, incidents, and loss. Most of the time, it's easy to get over this, to take control, move on. But if problems, or grief, overpower you and make you lose faith in who you are, and even what life is for, call on the power of this sigil to help you find wisdom, and even great insight, from the problems that have bound you.

Find Wisdom in Problems

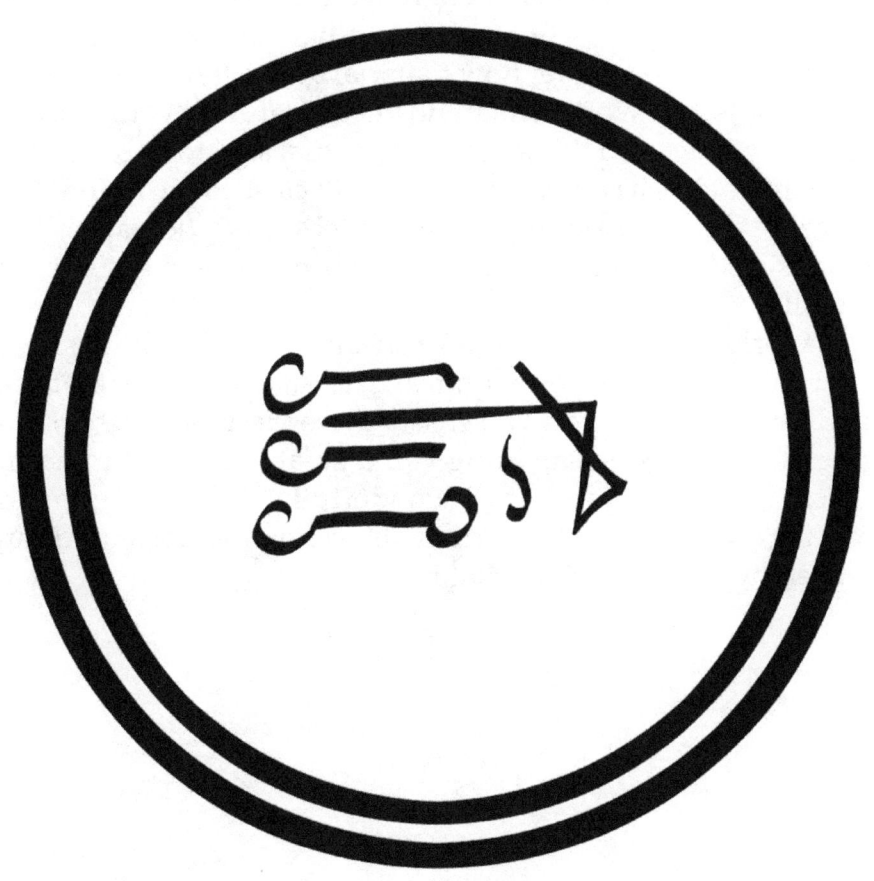

Discover Your True Passion

If you want to find out your true passion, you can't just do a quick bit of sigil magick and hope you hear a voice calling, 'You are going to be a famous opera singer.' This sigil is not even about your career – not necessarily. It's about finding something that, no matter how material or shallow it may seem, makes life seem worthwhile and meaningful to you. I knew somebody who used this so-called spiritual sigil to find out that she wanted to be a comedian. Somebody close to me found that he really wanted to build those model-train landscapes, but he'd resisted the idea since childhood because he'd assumed it was silly.

Working with this magick can uncover a lovely passion, but it can also make you admit to dreams and hopes that are startling, and once you've sensed these desires, it's hard to ignore them. Passion can bring you a great amount of mindful presence, of flow, and is a wonderfully spiritual act, and working with this sigil brings clues, revelations and an awakening to the passions that rouse you.

Discover Your True Passion

PERSONAL STRENGTH

As you get older, it's difficult to take your friends seriously when they say they're going on a diet, taking up exercise, throwing away the cigarettes or limiting their drinking to one glass of wine. That's not because people are weak, but because so many of the things we want to achieve, require immense personal strength. This section of the book starts with basic willpower but then elaborates on ways to break habits, get more done, as well as working with confidence and even addiction. The strength within you is greater than you can imagine, and these sigils give you access to that strength.

In this section, you will find sigils to Increase Willpower, Break a Habit, Overcome Procrastination, Find Relief from Addiction, Experience Self Confidence, and Finish What You Start.

Increase Willpower

You'll get the most out of this sigil if there's a reason you want to increase your willpower. You're giving up booze for a year? Great, you've got motivation. The beautiful thing about this ritual is that each time you use it, so long as there's a strong motivation, your overall willpower increases.

Increase Willpower

Break a Habit

If you've got a real addiction, see the addiction sigil. But if you've got an annoying habit, like biting your nails or being rude to your brother or forgetting the names of people you meet – use this sigil. It's not a general 'stop bad habits' sigil, so you need to use it on each habit that you want to break. And you have to want the change yourself, not just because somebody else has asked you to change.

Break a Habit

Overcome Procrastination

Procrastination is a complex problem, and there are long books written about it. You can spend a long time reading them and trying out the methods, or you can use this sigil. It's quicker. (Those books really might help, but you know, doing something *now* might be a good idea too.)

Overcome Procrastination

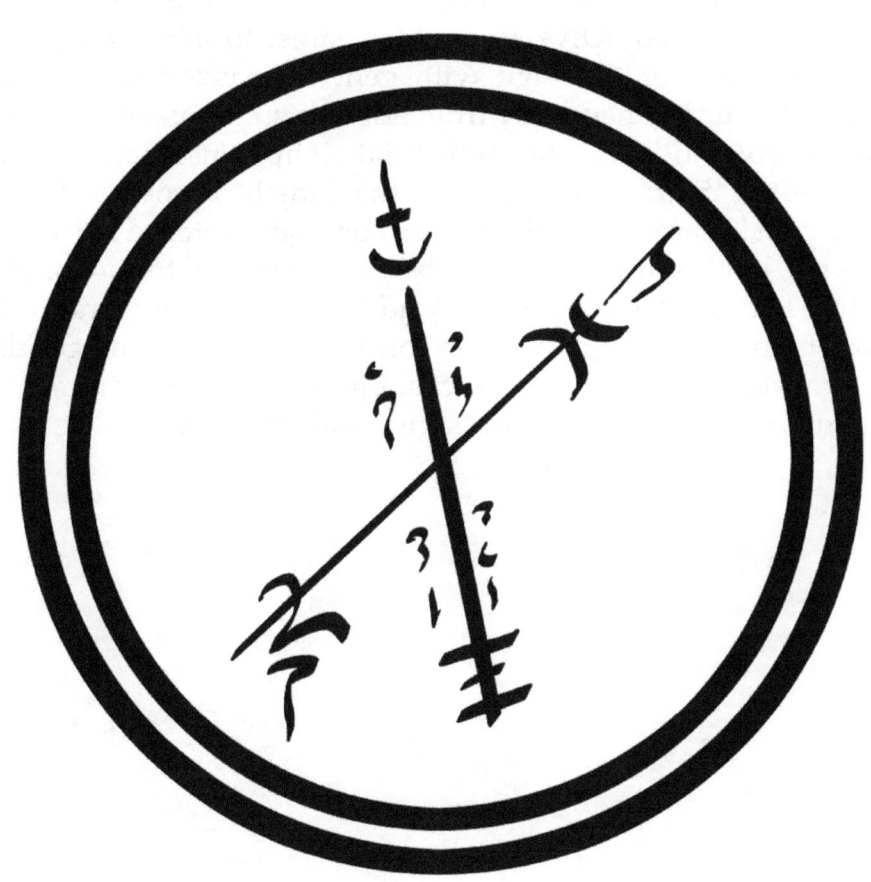

Find Relief from Addiction

I use the word relief because I'd be a fraud if I claimed that I could cure addiction. So I cannot promise to help you quit drugs – from caffeine to heroin. But if you're giving up anything that's addictive, from video games to substances, call on the power of this sigil with genuine passion and let it support your journey away from addiction. If you slip and go back to your addiction, remember that a slip is just that and not a disaster. Start again, repeat the ritual. Recovery from addiction is hard. Probably the most obvious sentence I've ever written, but it's important here, because you need to *know* that, before taking it on. And breaking addictions can put a strain on your body so you might want to consult your doctor and get all the conventional support you can. But make the commitment, use this sigil and let the magick give you true power.

Find Relief from Addiction

Experience Self-Confidence

This sigil can be used to build your confidence in a general way, or before a specific happening. Something curious we've noticed about this is that when it's used for a specific event, such as a wedding or when public speaking – the confidence can wax and wane. It never leaves you completely, but it's rarely at full power the whole time. If you're prepared for this, it's easier to cope with. And it's certainly better than not using the sigil at all.

Experience Self-Confidence

Finish What You Start

If you use the procrastination sigil, I bet you'll use this one too. From cleaning out the garden shed to finishing a year-long project, this sigil helps you finish something you've started. Use it when you feel like your motivation has dried up, and it will help you see the most efficient and enjoyable way to get everything done.

Finish What You Start

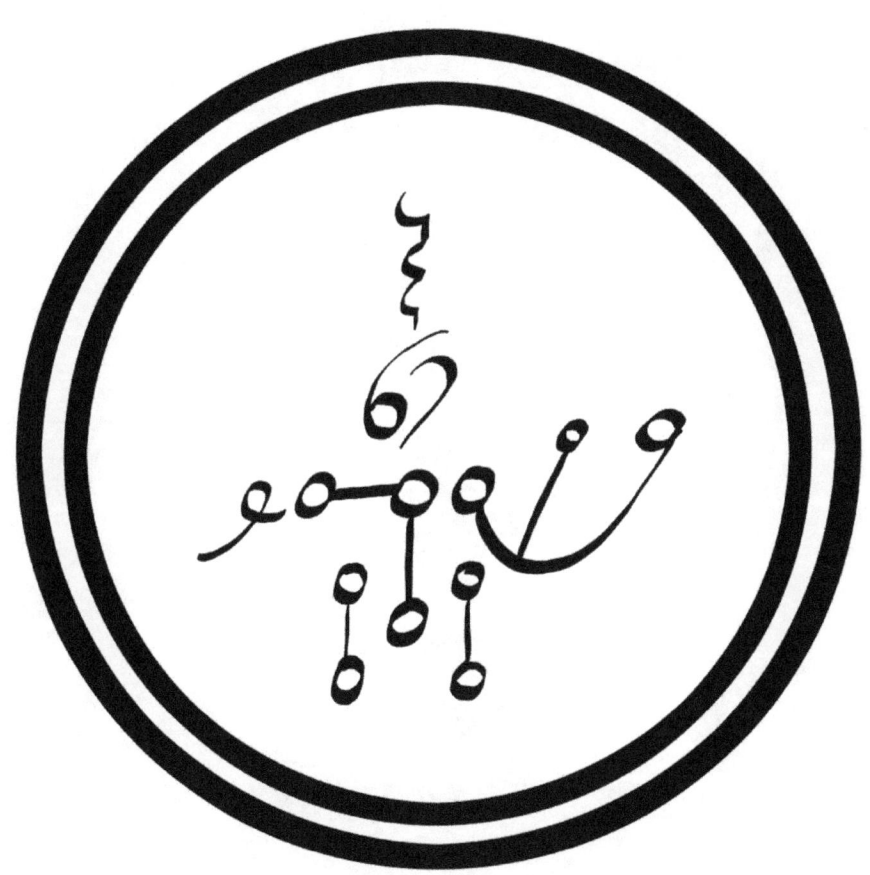

PEACE MAGICK

There are few things as beautiful as a sense of peace. The magick presented in this section can help you to cope with problems, finding peace within the storm, as well as solving problems, so that peace can return.

In this section, you will find sigils to Obtain Peace and Balance, Silence The Negative Voice, Ease the Pain of Memories, Banish Guilt and Shame, End Bad Luck, Heal a Damaged Relationship, Heal a Damaged Friendship, Heal a Damaged Work Relationship, End an Argument Peacefully, and Give Comfort and Peace.

Obtain Peace and Balance

When you feel overwhelmed, over-tired, or that you're too busy, too much in demand, this sigil can bring you peace. It's the one you turn to when you feel like you need a break but can't possibly see how you'll get one. The magick will help you settle within the circumstances, and can guide you to a more balanced existence. Some benefits can be felt quickly, but it can take some weeks or more to guide you to a place of true balance.

Obtain Peace and Balance

Silence the Negative Voice

If you suffer from negative self-chatter, use this sigil to silence the inner voice that tells you that you're doing it wrong, that everything will go wrong, and that there's no point. This can be used if you generally suffer from streams of negative thoughts, but can also be used as a one-off if something worries you and triggers a flow of these thoughts.

Silence the Negative Voice

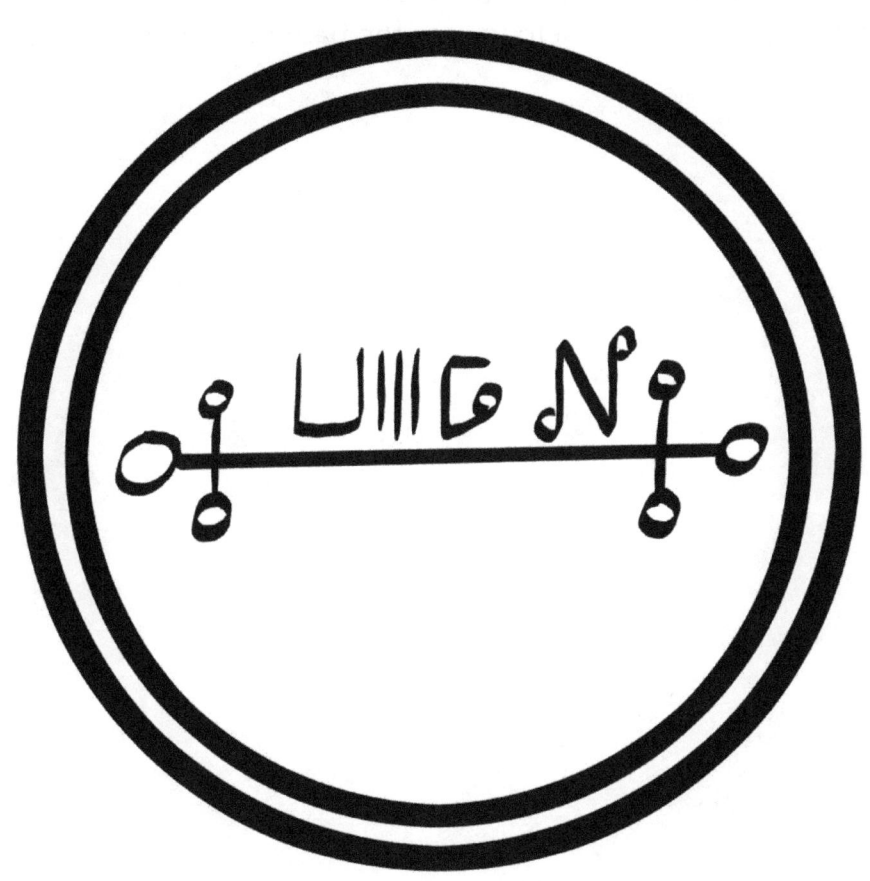

Ease the Pain of Memories

Grief and pain are a normal part of human existence, but if you find that some memories are still hurting you, long after they should have been defused, work with this sigil. It won't make you forget, but it can help to ease the pain that comes with the memory.

Ease the Pain of Memories

Banish Guilt and Shame

Sometimes we feel ashamed of very specific things we've done, and there's absolute guilt about specific actions. Sometimes, there's just a smoldering sense of guilt and shame. You can use this sigil on either form. If you know what you're feeling ashamed of, your desire is to ease the guilt and shame of those incidents. If you don't know what makes you feel a general sense of guilt or shame, then your desire is to let that feeling lift away, regardless of what causes it. Guilt and shame can be limiting, damaging, and unpleasant, and getting them to ease away can bring great peace.

Banish Guilt and Shame

End Bad Luck

If you feel that life has been unfair, that things are going wrong in a pattern, and that you're stuck in a cycle of misfortune, use this sigil. It's not there to lift a curse, but there are other causes of habitual misfortune. There's no need to get into the theory, but if you're having an undeniable run of bad luck, use this sigil. It's not going to solve all your problems by midnight. What it will do is stop the misfortune from developing, evolving, and growing. If anything else bad happens, that means it was already underway when you put this magick in place. But magick can work on the past as well as the future, so everything that happens from now should be less damaging. If bad luck's preventing you from getting on with life, bring it to an end with this sigil.

End Bad Luck

Heal a Damaged Relationship

Relationships get damaged all the time, through mistakes, casual asides, cruel actions that you regret, and even misunderstandings. Whatever the cause, and whether you're to blame or not, if you want healing – for both of you – use this sigil. It is aimed at romantic partnerships.

Heal a Damaged Relationship

Heal a Damaged Friendship

The description for this sigil could be almost identical to the previous sigil, but this one is for everybody except your romantic partner. Although you don't think of family members as friends, it saves us giving the sigil a long and complicated title. When a friendship (or non-romantic family relationship) has suffered, this sigil can bring healing. It can work even when there's minimal contact with the other party, and when the damage was caused long ago.

Heal a Damaged Friendship

Heal a Damaged Work Relationship

Work relationships are often fragile because you spend a lot of time with people who are sometimes almost strangers, sometimes best friends, sometimes competitors and sometimes those who have power over you. When a work relationship is strained or damaged, this sigil can bring healing, and helps you and the other party to return to more civil relations. If the other person is a complete enemy who's trying to undermine you, the next sigil in the book could be used first.

Heal a Damaged Work Relationship

End an Argument Peacefully

Arguments take so many forms; at home, work, and in any other environment. They can be caused by spite, pettiness, misunderstanding, or some underlying issue. When an argument is burning, simmering, or damaging your life in any way, use this sigil to bring peace. You may not win the argument, but you won't have to back down either. What you're looking for is peace, where nobody wants the friction to continue.

End an Argument Peacefully

Give Comfort and Peace

When somebody you know well is suffering, you often feel compelled to comfort them, and it can be so frustrating that words and actions barely seem to help. Use this sigil to send comfort and peace, in the form of loving compassion, right to the heart of the person you care about. This can bring peace in times of stress, grief, or any other form of unpleasantness.

Give Comfort and Peace

PROTECTION MAGICK

There are many forms of protection magick, and some will reduce your chance of being in an accident, or being harmed in any way, as well as repelling curses and preventing psychic attack. The rituals in this part of the book help banish negative energy, and can even cancel a curse. Sometimes, people curse you without magick – their pure hate leaves a mark. Even this kind of curse can be canceled out. When you're in a crisis, seeing a way out is often impossible, so there's a sigil for that, and there are some crafty ways to disarm enemies, make the unwanted move on and stop unpleasant people from harming you.

In this section, you will find sigils that include Banish Negative Energy, Cancel a Curse, Find a Pathway from Crisis, Protection Against Physical Violence, Protect Against Psychic Attack, Make Your Enemy Find Peace, Move from Anger to Peace, Remove Unwanted Attention, Discover Those Who Drain Your Energy, Ease People Out of Your Life, Make an Enemy Feel Compassion, Make an Enemy Sense Your Power, Bring Peace to a Home, and Make Noisy Neighbours Quiet.

Banish Negative Energy

Earlier in the book, there's a ritual to help remove the negative moods of those who are around you. This ritual is more for banishing negative energy that has no obvious cause. Sometimes, your home gets a creepy feeling. Or you may be traveling, and find yourself in a place that just doesn't feel right. There are more complex and careful ways to deal with this energy if you have the time and experience. It may be, for example, that the energy isn't actually negative or evil, but that it just doesn't mesh with your energy. Because of that, actually canceling it out might not be ideal. So although this is called a banishing, what it actually does is render the energy harmless to you. It provides a shield so that any benign entities are willing to ignore you, and any malevolent entities are unable to see you. If the energy comes from a person who is present, or who was present in the past, it will be removed even more rapidly.

Banish Negative Energy

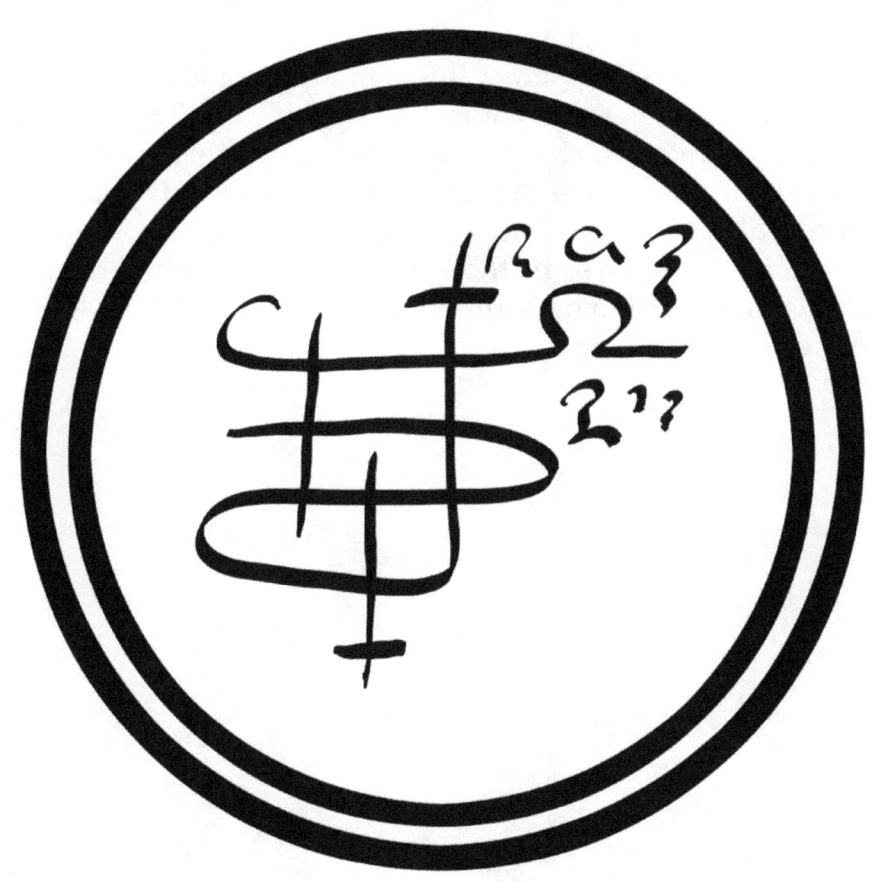

Cancel a Curse

In magick, there are many ways to cancel curses, but what I like about this one is that, because it doesn't call on angels or other spirits, it's able to work with curses from all styles of magick. In theory, angelic magick should be able to deal with anything, I know, but I have found that this sigil is great for dealing with casual curses, curses that come when people don't know your exact name, invented chaos curses, and curses that are derived from obscure traditions. Whatever, it works well. If you think you're cursed, you want rid of the curse, and this sigil can see it done in three days. In those unusual cases where a non-occultist has cursed you through pure hatred and ill will, this sigil will also work.

Cancel a Curse

Find a Pathway from Crisis

Life's going well, and then there's a crisis. This happens to everybody, regardless of how lucky, wealthy, or magickal they may be. It's part of life. The skill is to know how to respond. Often, when a crisis begins, we panic, pray, hope, or stick our head in the sand. Using this sigil is a better choice. I know of people who've been wrongly accused, charged for services they never received, and defrauded – and all emerged unscathed through bringing this sigil into play early on. Other magick is almost always involved, but this is where you get strength, clarity, and basic protection so that you remain clear-headed.

Find a Pathway from Crisis

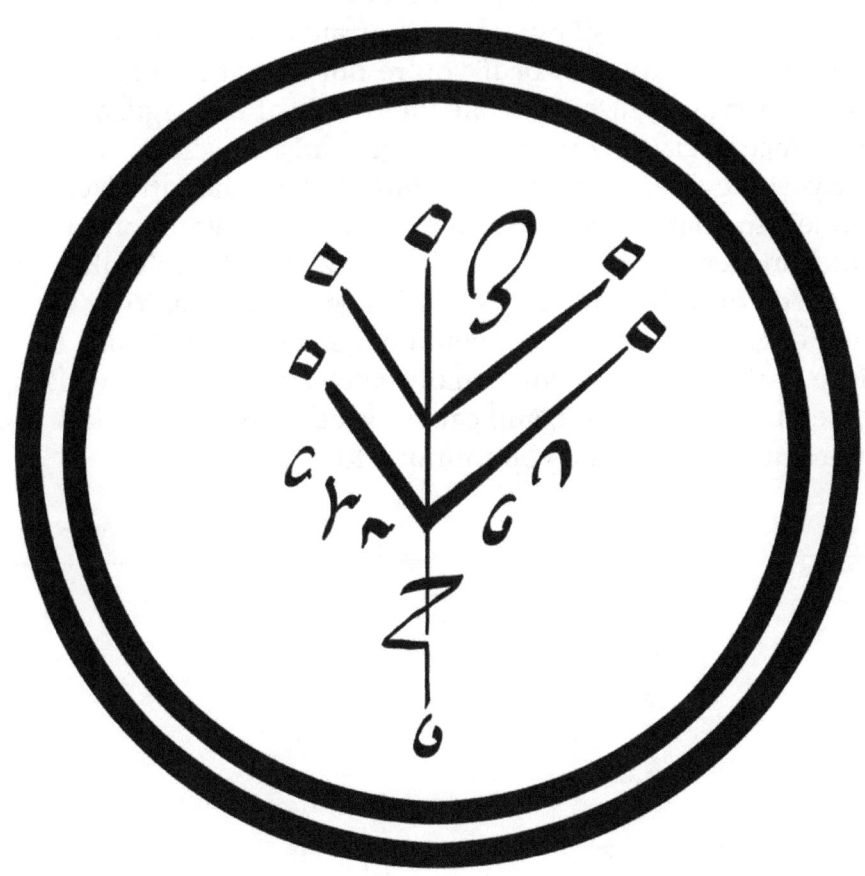

Protection Against Physical Violence

If you're in a situation where somebody known to you or close to you, threatens violence, this sigil is not going to help, and I can only suggest that you pursue every legal method you can to get out of there fast! But if you're afraid of violence when you go to particular places, or if you're out late at night – if it's a concern for any reason, invoke the power of this sigil. You can do it once every few months, for general protection. If you're going somewhere new that frightens you, the ritual can be applied to that specific journey. It will give you confidence, which makes you less vulnerable to attack, but don't take risks because you think the magick will keep you safe. Your usual level of caution and all conventional safeguards should be in place at all times. So if you usually catch a cab to avoid walking somewhere unpleasant, still catch the cab. The sigil makes you safer but doesn't make you immune to attack.

Protection Against Physical Violence

Protect Against Psychic Attack

Psychic attack can leave you feeling weak, confused, even unwell. If somebody has it in for you, put up your defenses with this sigil. It even works once an attack is fully underway. You don't need to know the source of the attack, or even if an attack is definitely happening. If you suspect you're under attack, use this ritual to find relief, and you will get the relief you seek.

Protect Against Psychic Attack

Make Your Enemy Find Peace

The most cunning way to defeat your enemy is to make them feel at peace. This ritual works in several ways, bringing a sleepy calm when your enemy thinks about you, along with a disarming mix of positive emotions. It also makes your enemy feel weak and in need of comfort. Somehow, this cocktail of effects means that an obsessed enemy, who's been out to get you, will lose interest in you. Often, the enemy will become positively warm to you. It's a strange sigil, and it brings peace to your enemy via a highly indirect route, but it brings peace to them, and thus to you.

Make Your Enemy Find Peace

Move from Anger to Peace

Earlier in the book, I talked about anger as an energy that you can use. That's fine until anger becomes something that you're afraid of, something that damages you and makes you feel out of control. If your anger reaches these levels, you need protection from yourself. Seek peace with this sigil.

Move from Anger to Peace

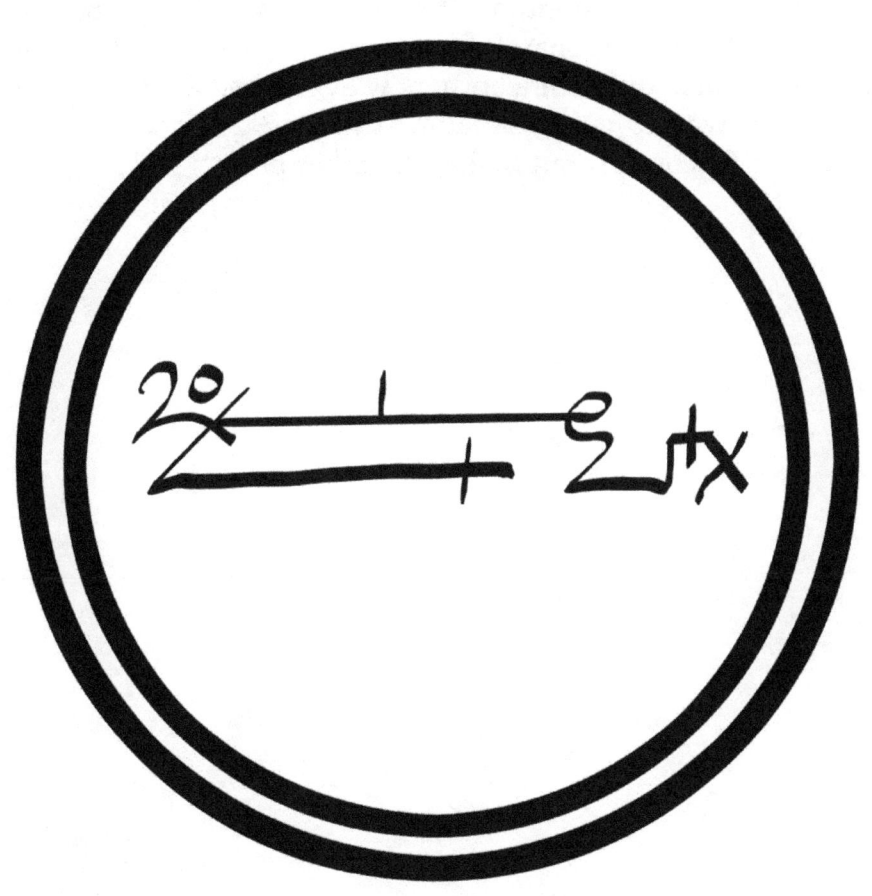

Remove Unwanted Attention

You might be pestered online, at work, or even by somebody in your own home. If you need privacy, this sigil will help to remove unwanted attention. If somebody's actively obsessed with you, the effects may be temporary, but for mild stalker-types who latch onto somebody new every few weeks, this can be a great way to get some alone-time back. It doesn't cause enmity or discomfort but makes the other person feel complete without you.

Remove Unwanted Attention

Discover Those Who Drain Your Energy

Knowledge is protection, and if somebody is draining your energy, deliberately or simply by being that kind of person, you need to know. Work this ritual, with the desire to find out who drains you, and you will become aware of it when you are in that person's presence. All friends make you tired – but what I'm talking about is the sort of person who *really* saps your energy, makes you feel negative and leaves you feeling a little beaten. Sometimes it's obvious, but other times you sense there's a person like this, and you have no idea who it is. Finding out the culprit is the first step to curing the problem.

Discover Those Who Drain Your Energy

Ease People Out of Your Life

When you want somebody to move out of your life, there are many ways to tackle it, and the most straightforward is to end the relationship or friendship. Often, this can feel really uncomfortable, so you need an alternative. With relationships, I think you owe the other person some honesty, but in those strained, strange and weird friendships, or when there is a cloying neighbor or a weird co-worker, magick can help that person to move on. You might find a string of coincidences make that person move away completely, but often they'll just lose interest. If you have a housemate you want to get rid of, this can trigger the move, but I have to be honest and say that when the person lives with you, this sigil is a bit less likely to work. Still worth trying!

Ease People Out of Your Life

Make an Enemy Feel Compassion

A few pages ago, there was a sigil to make your enemy find peace. This one is similar but helps the enemy feel compassion for you. It's more direct and can bring a stronger result, but the catch is that it's less likely to work. As with so many of these, it's worth a try, and can even be used at the same time as the other sigil. It works well in divorces and other situations where the person once cared about you.

Make an Enemy Feel Compassion

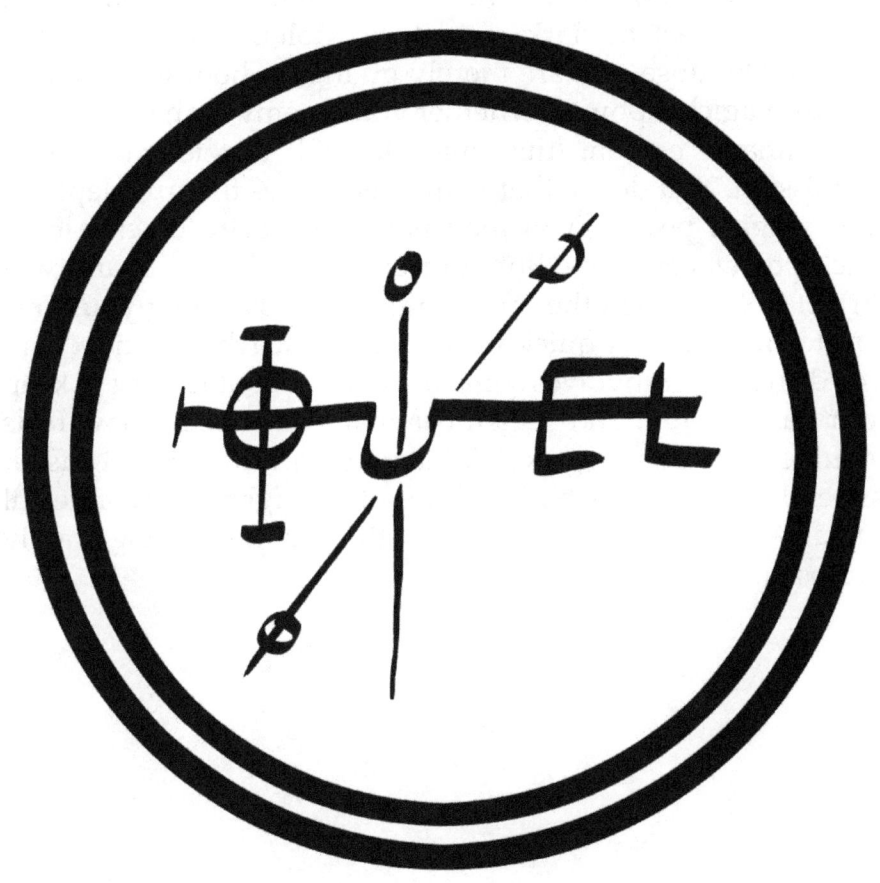

Make an Enemy Sense Your Power

If you are facing a truly cruel and dangerous enemy, somebody who wants to break you and damage your reputation or harm you in other ways, you may need to frighten that person. Doing so is not an act of dark magick or violence, but quite the opposite, because you are merely giving an honest revelation of your magickal power. Whether your enemy is an occultist or an ordinary person, this magick will dazzle them into submission. You desire that your enemy sees the true depth of your magick power. You may not even begin to sense how much power you have. But your enemy *will* sense it and will shrivel in fear when they next think about harming you. This can stop attacks very quickly. You may notice that the next real-world encounter involves some uneasy eye contact. Try to keep your gaze steady, and remember that your enemy now feels genuine fear. This magick is in no way dark or evil, because it is merely letting somebody glimpse the bright and wonderful human spirit within you, and that is something rarely glimpsed.

Make an Enemy Sense Your Power

Bring Peace to a Home

When your home feels disrupted, filled with aggression or continual arguments, you may need more than the earlier sigil to improve the mood of others. This sigil works to ensure that the home is protected from outside forces (of whatever nature!) and that the individuals within the home connect to their deepest sense of peace. I've seen this make the wildest households become pleasant in a matter of minutes. Sadly, it doesn't always work that fast, but it really does work.

Bring Peace to a Home

Make Noisy Neighbors Quiet

Noisy neighbors drive you crazy, and shutting them up can be difficult. They may leave their dog barking all night. They may play loud music. They may scream at each other, or shout in the street. Often, your only hope is to move away or wait until they do. It is worth trying this sigil because it works more than half the time. When it works, it works amazingly well, without harming anybody. Give it a try. If it works, great. You may need to repeat it when they get noisy again.

If it doesn't work, consider using other magick in this book, such as *Banish Negative Energy, Make Your Enemy Find Peace, Ease People Out of Your Life, Make an Enemy Feel Compassion, Make an Enemy Sense Your Power* and *Bring Peace to a Home*. You can shape all these rituals, so they are aimed at your noisy neighbors. If you do all this and it fails, you're going to think magick is pretty useless, so I have to say, of all the magick I've worked with, this is one of the least predictable. When this works, what a joy. You hear stories of people moving away within days when it looked like they'd be there for centuries. Others just calm down. But I hear just as many stories of frustration, where the noise continues. Try not to think about that. Trust this sigil, and give it a go.

Make Noisy Neighbors Quiet

PERSONAL HEALING

This part of the book covers several psychological issues such as anxiety and depression, and I cannot say it strongly enough that (even though conventional treatment can be a disappointingly long journey) you must seek conventional treatment for all such issues. If you throw away your meds and rely on magick, you could end up in serious trouble. But if you believe in magick, and if you want another way to help work with these issues, I have a lot of faith in this magick.

Although this section is about healing yourself, I also look at bitterness, jealousy, and other states that you might not think of as things that need to be healed. But they do. If you let these aspects of yourself fester, they make you unwell, from the soul to the skin.

In this section, you will find sigils to Overcome Anxiety, Banish Fear and Worry, Ease Depression, Quieten the Mind, Lighten Your Mood, Overcome Bitterness, and Release the Pain of Jealousy.

Overcome Anxiety

This sigil can be used before a one-off event that makes you anxious, before flying, before an exam, anything like that. It can be used if you feel general anxiety or suffer from episodes of panic that seem to come on without obvious triggers. For events that make most people anxious, such as flying, it's been seen to work extremely well. For more long-term anxiety, it's a bit more unpredictable. Some say it helps reduce the number and intensity of episodes. Usually, it makes an initial and obvious difference, but then as you repeat it every few weeks, or whenever you feel the need, the improvements are more gradual.

Overcome Anxiety

Banish Fear and Worry

Worrying about things can drain you, and leave you feeling emotionally wrecked and quite unwell. Fear is a natural part of our existence, but chronic fear can be invasive and destructive. If you're afraid too much of the time, fretting and worrying when things usually turn out OK, use this sigil to help you let go of the worrying thoughts and the obsessive fears. It can bring great peace.

Banish Fear and Worry

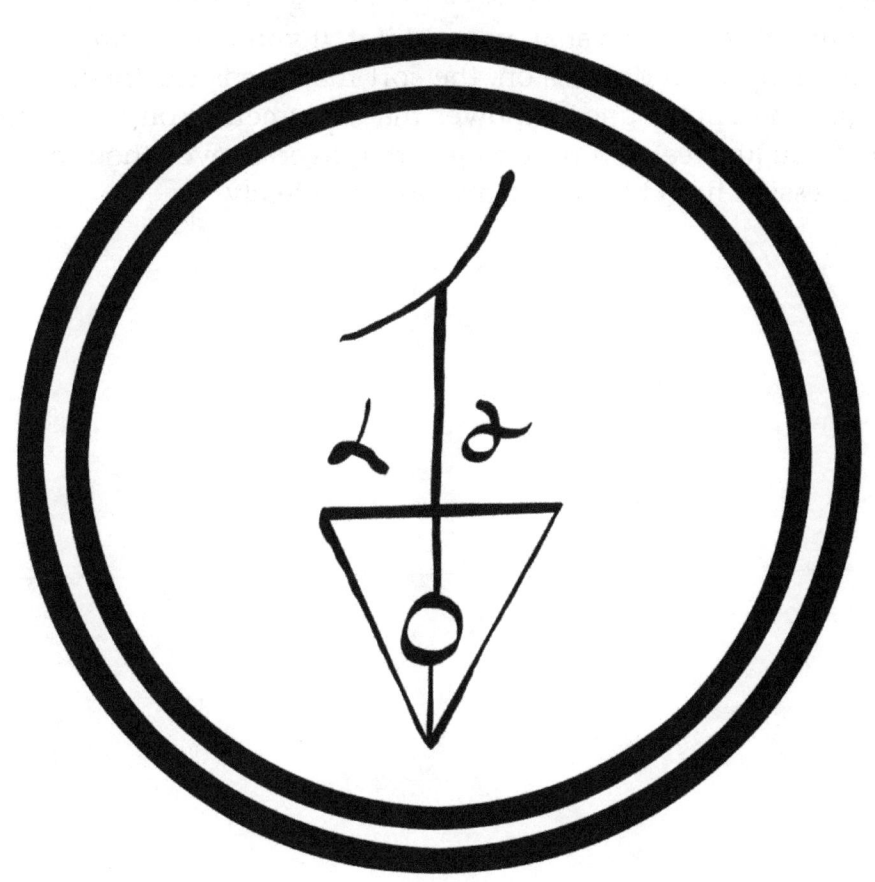

Ease Depression

As with many of the sigils in this book, this can be used in two ways. If you're just having a down week, where things have got on top of you, and you feel they're making you lower than they should, this sigil can snap you out if it. If you're suffering from more long-term depression, the sort that needs treatment, the sigil can support and empower that treatment. You may find that you just feel you're coping better, overall, even though the depression hasn't been taken away completely.

Ease Depression

Quieten the Mind

When your mind's racing, it can feel overwhelming. Or you may just find that your mind feels too busy, and although it's not a big deal you want a slightly calmer existence. This sigil can help to bring peace to your thoughts, without meditation, and without dulling your consciousness. If you do meditate, you can use this to get to a deeper state more rapidly.

Quieten the Mind

Lighten Your Mood

This sigil isn't about depression, but anger, frustration, and other negative moods that make you feel too stormy and snappy at other people. If you've fallen into this sort of rut, the sigil can bring you relief quite rapidly. If you get the relief you want after one or two days, there's no need to complete the full three days of the ritual.

Lighten Your Mood

Overcome Bitterness

When you're bitter, it's like being filled with acid, and it eats away at your health. Obsessive bitterness can make you physically unwell, and weaken your ability to love and trust. Bitterness can feel justified because you've been wronged, but letting that bitterness stay with you is only a punishment to yourself. If you can see this, and if you're tired of bitterness making you feel so uptight, use this sigil to let go of those feelings.

Overcome Bitterness

Release the Pain of Jealousy

There are many ways to be jealous. You might want what somebody else has, or you might be plagued by mistrust of a partner. Whatever form jealousy takes, it's not good for you. It is a form of pain. It can ruin relationships and scrapes away at your mental health, sometimes for years. If you relieve that pain and remove the jealousy, you'll be able to see your genuine needs more clearly, and in relationships, you'll find it easier to communicate about whatever's bothering you. Notice how awful jealousy makes you feel, and use this sigil to take that feeling away.

Release the Pain of Jealousy

HEALTH MAGICK

Health magick is a slippery subject. There should be caution, restraint, no big promises of instant cures. There are too many medical frauds in the world, from giant corporations to fake healers. I can only offer health magick to you if it's something I genuinely believe in. It has to work, or it isn't in the book. I can't guarantee it will work every time, but everything you find here – we know it works. From experience.

The magick presented here is an offer of a possibility, not the promise of a miracle. If the potential for recovery is within you, magick can release that potential.

I can't go further without this story. A few short years ago, I had two friends with cancer. They both became ill around the same time, purely by coincidence. Both of them accepted extensive and unpleasant chemotherapy. One friend used magick, to heal and support. The magick did support her, but after several months of suffering, she died.

The other friend did not die, even though she used no magick. She's still alive today. Perhaps that's not the inspiring story you expected.

This doesn't make me cynical but puts everything in perspective. I don't believe in fate, and I don't believe that when your number's up, it's up, because I know angels have saved people in the middle of violent accidents. Magick can save lives. But I also know that health magick is unpredictable. It brings comfort, support, and healing, and I have faith in this or why put it in the book, right?

Let this magick give you hope. People suffer pain, and they die, and sometimes the best medicine and best magick does nothing. But every member of The Gallery of Magick has agreed that it would be wrong to withhold our knowledge. We have magickal knowledge that can help with pain, discomfort, and some more minor health issues, and it feels like our absolute duty to share that with you.

In this section, you will find sigils to Discover the Willpower to Eat Well, Reduce Your Appetite Through the Joy of Eating, Uncover the Motivation to Exercise, Heal Sore Bones and Joints, Recover from Stomach Sickness, Ease Chronic Pain, Cope with Symptoms, Recover Rapidly from Colds and Flu, Make You Skin Glow with Health, Heal with Loving Light, Encourage Deep Sleep, Release the Energy of Youthfulness, and Sharpen Your Mind.

Discover the Willpower to Eat Well

This sigil doesn't sound like much but could be the most important health magick you ever do. You don't need me to lecture you about the importance of eating well. If you're well, it's an integral part of staying well and living long. If you're not well, or uncomfortable with the weight you carry, eating well can restore much-needed balance. Good eating becomes a habit, in just a few weeks, but it can take willpower to get there. Use this sigil to give you the willpower, and top up every few days or weeks, if you feel you're slipping back into bad habits.

Discover the Willpower to Eat Well

Reduce Your Appetite Through the Joy of Eating

You probably already think you've got plenty of joy when it comes to eating. How can it reduce your appetite? That old advice to eat slowly and chew your food over and over – it's good advice. Unconsciously shoveling food down while watching a movie or driving or doing anything else, means you don't taste, feel, or enjoy the food. That means you can stuff a lot more in there. When you really slow down and savor the food, you find that you fill up on *less* food. This doesn't happen overnight if you're living off junk food, but it does happen. This sigil can help you bring your focus to eating. You can think of eating as a ritual practice of nourishment, where you bless and adore the food. Sounds a bit whacky, but when you really focus on the taste and texture and how full you feel, you eat less. The principal is covered in loads of mindfulness books, and other places, so the idea is nothing new. But using magick to help raise your awareness does make a difference.

Reduce Your Appetite Through the Joy of Eating

Uncover The Motivation to Exercise

You're not generating the motivation – you're uncovering it. When you watch little kids play, you wonder where they get their energy. But adults can be as active and energy-filled if we get past the notion that we need another sit-down and a cup of tea. Getting into exercise when you're utterly sedentary isn't easy, because you're meant to consult your doctor, start slowly, be very careful about warming up and going slowly to avoid injuries. It can be really tough to find the time and the motivation. This sigil helps with the motivation. It gets you fired up, and if you feel laziness creeping back in, the sigil can get you going again. If you already exercise, but not as often as you want, the sigil can boost your motivation a bit.

Uncover The Motivation to Exercise

Find More Physical Energy

If you get out of breath walking up a flight of stairs, this sigil can't help. You need to do something about your physical fitness and stamina. See the previous sigil. But if you're suffering from unexplained fatigue, constant tiredness and the sort of malaise that doctors say they can't help you with, this sigil can bring back some of your physical energy. It works in two ways. You get a direct increase in energy; it can come on rapidly or grow over a few days. You also might get intuitions about what's sapping your energy; certain foods, habits and so on. I won't say too much about this second aspect, because I don't want to give ideas that shape what you experience. But be open to intuition. It might not happen, but you might get little nudges of thought that make you realize there are changes you can make that affect your levels of physical energy.

Find More Physical Energy

Heal Sore Bones and Joints

The healing brought by this sigil is largely pain relief. If you've actually broken a bone or injured a joint, some claim this can speed the healing process. My experience of the sigil is that it can reduce pain. Never give up your conventional treatments, but use this sigil alongside them. If you have unexplained bone or joint pain, that doctors can't explain or help with, then seek relief with this sigil.

Heal Sore Bones and Joints

Recover from Stomach Sickness

If you get stomach sickness, you'll usually get better all on your own, without any magick. But this sigil can speed the rehabilitation. It's also been used by people who have ongoing, unexplained stomach symptoms. If the doctors have done every test imaginable, and you still feel nauseous, or your stomach gurgles uncomfortably, use this sigil to seek relief.

Recover from Stomach Sickness

Ease Chronic Pain

If I could cure chronic pain, I'd be a billionaire, but this sigil is offered because I have seen it bring relief to those who've been unable to find anything that works. It can work when there's pain that you understand, from a known cause. It's also effective for those mysterious and stubborn pains that fill the body and leave doctors skeptical or bemused.

Ease Chronic Pain

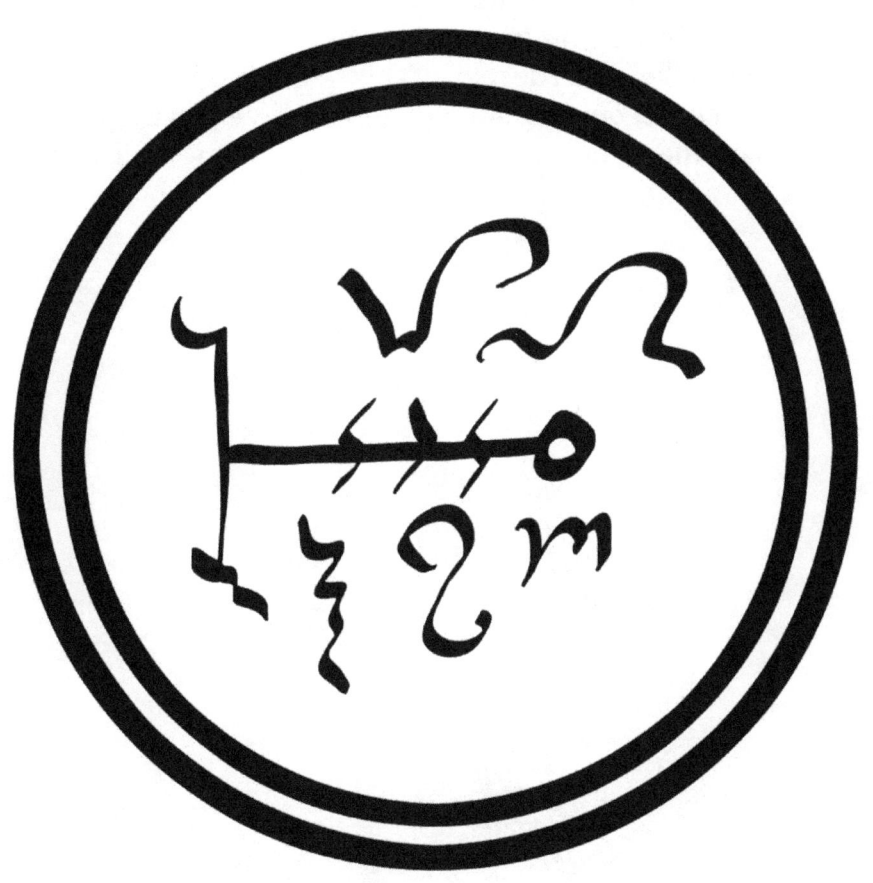

Cope with Symptoms

It's not pleasant, but sometimes you get ill and stay ill, or you have to endure some ongoing treatment, and it sucks. If you're in that sort of place, where the doctors have told you to toughen up and get through the next few weeks as well as you can, it can really make you despair. This sigil might reduce the symptoms a little, but its main power is to give you the strength to cope with the symptoms while you have them, until they are gone.

Cope with Symptoms

Recover Rapidly from Colds and Flu

If you get a cold or the flu, you need to follow all the conventional advice. You'll get better in a few days, or sometimes in a couple of weeks. This sigil aids recovery by giving you more energy, reducing the impact of the symptoms and by making your rest more restorative. It's not a direct cure, but an aid to recovery.

Recover Rapidly from Colds and Flu

Make Your Skin Glow with Health

Sometimes you turn up at a party, and somebody says, 'Oh, you look so young and healthy. What have you been doing?' and you've been doing nothing. Other times, you turn up feeling fine, and everybody asks, 'Are you quite well?' It makes you feel like you must look old and feeble. I've never understood how this works, in scientific terms, but I know it can be affected by inner energy and the way we project that energy. It's not your actual skin that's glowing with health – it's *you* that's shining through your skin. So that's what this sigil does. It's not plastic surgery. You won't actually look younger in photographs, but when people encounter you in person, you can expect compliments.

Make Your Skin Glow with Health

Heal with Loving Light

You can offer to heal others, even if you've never tried before. Use this sigil for three days beforehand, working on your desire to heal – you don't need to have a specific person in mind, only know that you want to have the power to heal. Then, at any time after the ritual, with the other person's permission, you lay your hand over the place that is causing the problem. There are many techniques you can use now – such as imagining white light going in, and dark matter being pulled out. All these things work. But with this sigil, we've found it can be as simple as placing your hand there with the intention of healing. That's all you do. Let your hand stay over the affected area for a few minutes, and *know* that it's bringing relief to the other person. It might take practice to get good at this. You're not going to cure cancer, and sometimes you won't even be able to take a headache away, but this remarkably simple approach to healing can bring relief. Some people have used this technique on themselves, and they find relief. That has never worked for me, but why not try?

Heal with Loving Light

Encourage Deep Sleep

Insomnia can be an indication of many other physical and psychological problems, so shouldn't be taken lightly. But if you want to add magick, this sigil is a potent way to find relief. If you've suffered from long-term insomnia, perform the ritual, forget about it, and sometime in the future, you may notice a difference. When you do, repeat the ritual, attempting to get even deeper and more predictable sleep. If you're not an insomnia sufferer, but find yourself all hyped up and unable to sleep (due to a hectic day or an upcoming event that stresses you out of your mind), you can use this ritual just once (rather than for three days), and it can ease you to sleep. If you're not really an insomniac but have developed bad sleep habits, the sigil can help break them.

Encourage Deep Sleep

Release the Energy of Youthfulness

Earlier in the book, there's a sigil for increased physical energy, but this sigil is more about that youthful feeling where you feel alert, motivated, and eager to be on the move. If you're slumped in your chair, losing interest and feeling old and stiff, this is the sigil that can get you moving. It might be that you want to walk a bit more, or that you're taking up hiking again, or just that you want to get through social occasions without snoozing. If you feel older than you want to feel, let this sigil give you back some of that youthful energy.

Release the Energy of Youthfulness

Sharpen Your Mind

After a hard working life, my mother retired in a big way and wanted to do nothing but sit in front of the TV. Within a couple of years, I could see her mind losing its edge. We made her read a book once a week, and do the newspaper crossword every day, whether she liked it or not. And it worked. She sharpened her mind. I don't know about you, but I felt like after the age of twenty-five I'd peaked mentally, and (far sooner than expected) I started forgetting names, directions, why I'd walked into a certain room. It happens to us all, and what starts as a mildly amusing annoyance soon becomes a bit worrying. Is my brain really going rotten already? I was fine, but my mind was just a bit dull compared to when I was twenty-one. My advice, obviously, is to keep your mind busy and active, from your twenties to your nineties, and beyond. But if you find that you lack the energy or willpower to do that, or that you're just feeling mentally foggy, forgetful and sluggish, use this sigil. It can be used quite generally, to give you a few months of extra focus, or it can be used before an event where you want to keep the brightness of your mind in sharp focus.

Sharpen Your Mind

WISDOM AND EDUCATION

I had a friend who left school early because he wanted to get a job. He told me, years later, that he left because he thought he'd fail. I knew he was clever, but he had no idea. Off he went to learn a trade, and his intelligence was never recognized by his employers. It was obvious to me at the time that all he needed was a good teacher, and the time to learn, and in a few years he'd have been able to enter his profession at a higher level than he ever achieved. Because of this sad story, I am big on education. Doesn't mean we all have to be clever and extraordinary, but with the right teacher, an ability to learn, organize, and pass exams, you can achieve more than you realize. This is true even if you're changing jobs, starting a new career, or taking up a hobby.

In this section, you will find sigils to Learn With Ease, Pass Exams Easily, Develop a New Skill Easily, Improve Organisational Skills, and Find a Great Teacher.

Learn with Ease

Preparing for an exam, undertaking a long course or any time where you're gathering information, this sigil works in two ways. It helps you understand more rapidly (by connecting the information to things you already know), and it helps you recall more easily. If you're studying for years, use it once a month or so, focusing on your desire to learn the next chunk of knowledge that's being directed at you. For an exam, do the three-day ritual before you begin your revision.

Learn with Ease

Pass Exams Easily

You're not going to pass an exam easily unless you do the work and learn your subject. That's not a disclaimer, but common sense. If that annoys you, sorry, but this magick is not going to help you cheat the system. But if you've put in the work, this sigil will make sure you are calm, creative, with clear recollection during your exam. Works for written exams as well as driving tests and other performance-based exams. I've heard of it being used for auditions, because to singers, actors and other performers, auditions feel like an exam. Use the sigil in the days just before your exam. If you can perform the ritual on the exam day, that's great, but any time near to the date of the exam will be OK.

Pass Exams Easily

Develop a New Skill Easily

Any time you're learning a new skill, from juggling to computer-coding, you will learn faster when you use this sigil. It's aimed at skills, rather than pure knowledge, so that's where you actually *do* something with the knowledge. It might be photography, skateboarding, rock-climbing, chess - anything where you learn and do.

Develop a New Skill Easily

Improve Organizational Skills

This works at home, work or anywhere you need to be better organized, but it's more about getting organized over a long period of time, and changing habits, than just sorting out one problem. It's been used by people running large projects, such as people in the arts and television, as well as promotions and other management projects where lots of people need to be looked after. It's also used to keep home offices running smoothly, or to make a business more efficient.

The sigil works best on long-term organization, so isn't there to help you with packing your suitcases, but when you need to feel calm control on a larger scale, it works readily.

Improve Organizational Skills

Find a Great Teacher

A good teacher can save you hundreds (or thousands) of hours. Not to mention dollars. Need a good driving instructor or somebody to teach you how to sail, or is passing your exams seriously important to you? This works best when you're trying to source an individual – one person who can help you learn. You won't find the cheapest or most convenient teacher, but you will find one who works best for you. Teachers may appear in surprising ways, through chance meetings and introductions. But it may just be that you see an advertisement that catches your eye. Use your intuition.

It says 'teacher' up there, but we've found this sigil can even be used when you need help from all sorts of professionals, from dentists to psychiatrists and accountants. It works best if your need is quite strong, rather than casual. If you need six dental implants, your need is real, and finding the right person to get you through that is important.

Find a Great Teacher

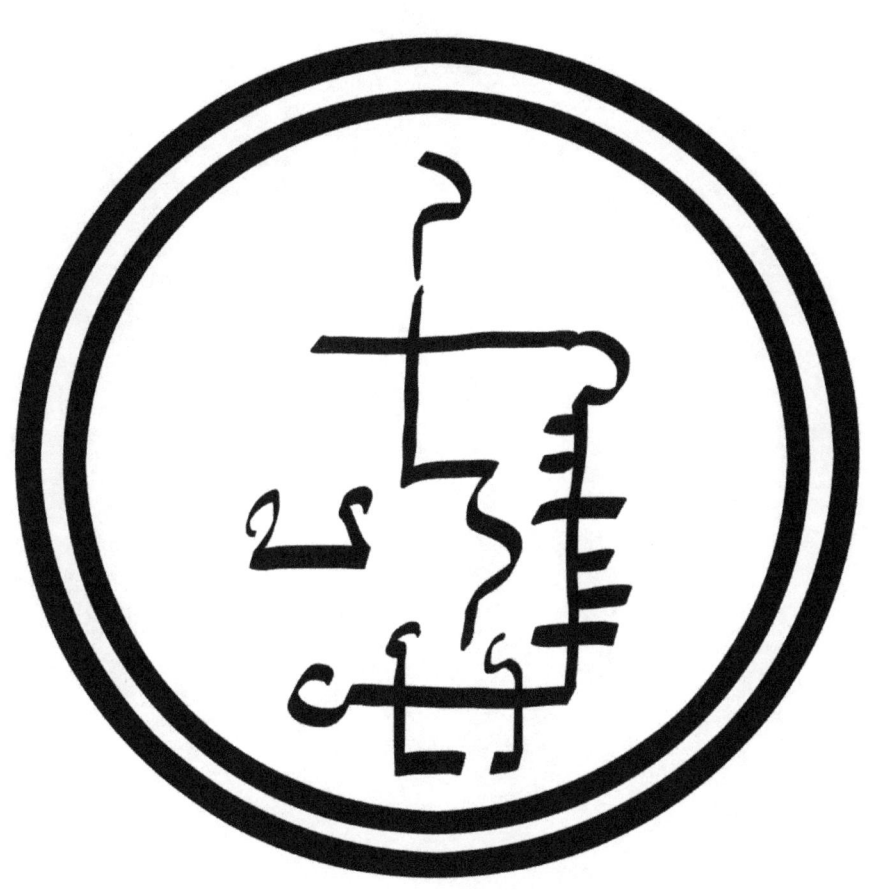

BUSINESS AND FINANCE

Money magick makes some people squirm with discomfort when there's guilt about materialism and greed. If you don't like it, don't use it. But if you feel like you want things to go better, get comfortable with that and allow this financial magick to work.

In this section, you will find sigils including the Business Booster, Raise Money for Your Projects, Money from Out of the Blue, Steady Income Increase, Make Your Money Go Further, and Enjoy Spending and Sharing.

Business Booster

If you run a business, you want it to do well all the time, and this sigil is just what you need. If things are OK, you probably want them to be better, so use the sigil to give your business an overall boost. You don't have to be too specific, and it's best if you're not. You might find, through intuition or an unusual coincidental incident, exactly what you need to change to improve business. Or things may just happen that make business better.

If you're struggling, if your business is suffering, you can target the magick more directly at a perceived problem. It takes some skill to know what's damaging your business, but if you know where the problem lies, target the magick at boosting that aspect of your business.

Business Booster

Raise Money for Your Projects

This works whether you need a home loan, money for a business startup, or even when you're doing that crowdfunding thing, where you politely ask people to support your album release/trip around the world/short film directing debut. If you've got a project, and it needs money, this is the sigil to use. Don't sit back and wait for cash. Get up and do something to raise the money, but know the magick will help.

Raise Money for Your Projects

Money from Out of the Blue

Everybody loves money from out of the blue. When you use this, don't expect money to get slipped under your door. The results can be easily missed. Sometimes, you get charged less than you expected. Or you get given something you were going to buy. It's not as thrilling as a wad of notes, but hey, it's not bad. When you perform this ritual, you may want a set amount, because you have to pay a bill, or because you want to buy something specific. Cool, you can think about that amount. But you might get more or way less.

Whatever turns up, be grateful. But expect the best! And if you don't have a set amount in mind, that's even cooler. Just get that vibe of money turning up out of nowhere. Give it time. It can work in seconds, or it might take weeks. The less you stress about it, the better. If you only get $5 the first time you try it – well, that's because money magick is plain weird. It can take time to get it moving, because of all your guilt and hang-ups. So be glad for what you get and do it again. But don't do it every three days hoping to get rich. It's not a get rich quick scheme. It's for an occasional burst of money when you feel the need.

Money from Out of the Blue

Steady Income Increase

This is one of those sigils that really does work in a slow and steady way, bringing more money very gradually. It's not used when you need rapid cash, but because it's slow and gentle, it can be one of the more effective kinds of financial magick. You only need to work this once every few months, or even once a year, with the desire for your income to keep going up. If you have a steady job with set pay, you might get extra gifts and surprises. If you work in sales or business, your personal achievements might creep up. It can also just smooth away some money problems so that when you look back, you see you're better off than you were before. Doesn't seem very exciting, but it's a useful sigil if you're patient.

Steady Income Increase

Make Your Money Go Further

There are many versions of this ritual, found in many styles of magick, and yet it's really underused. It's like you're saying, 'No, no, I don't want my money to go further, I want MORE money or nothing.' OK, you get nothing. I'm only joking, but it really makes sense to work with this ritual, because a bit of financial luck goes a long way. You can use it when all's well, or when you're running out of money. The results we hear about come in many forms – somebody lets you off a debt, you get given money, something costs less than you thought, you find an old bank account has money in it, you get a tax return. This one doesn't always work fast, but the effect can last for months.

Make Your Money Go Further

Enjoy Spending and Sharing

Money has to flow, and if you feel tense and tight-fisted when you pay for anything – whether it's taxes or an ice-cream sundae - you can strangle the flow of money. If this describes you, use this sigil to make it feel better when you spend. This can unlock so much potential and makes all money magick more likely to work. Don't go spending on credit to feel good – all you're doing there is putting off the payment. Use this when money is actually leaving you forever. But let the magick reframe that, so it feels like money is flowing through you.

Same applies to sharing. You can share your money with family, with charities, with strangers. Doing it when you hate doing it makes you feel bad and stops the money flow. If you want to give, but always feel bad when you give, use this sigil to break open the damn, so that giving feels good. When giving feels good, receiving happens a lot more often.

Enjoy Spending and Sharing

EMPLOYMENT MAGICK

Work is such a huge part of your life, so working with magick to get the most out of your work is a solid approach. There are two communication rituals in this section, and they can be adapted whenever you need clear communication, anywhere in life. But we've found they work best in employment situations, so that's why they're in this part of the book.

In this section, you will find sigils to Attract a Promotion, Attract a Job That Suits Your Needs, Perform Well at Interview, Be Noticed by People of Importance, Communicate Clearly, and Communicate to a Group.

Attract a Promotion

You might be in line for a promotion so you can use this sigil to make sure it happens. Or it could be that you feel promotion is long overdue. If so, use this sigil to get noticed and appreciated, and to negotiate the deal you want.

Attract a Promotion

Attract a Job That Suits Your Needs

This is a multi-purpose sigil. You can use it when you're looking for a job that suits your needs, and then you can use it during the application and interview process to improve your chances. I have never used this sigil myself, because I'm self-employed, but I've seen what it does, and it's a good one.

As soon as you start looking for work (even if you're already employed), you can use this ritual to find a job that suits your needs. The word 'needs' doesn't just mean it's going to get you a job that pays the bills. It goes a bit deeper, so you're more likely to find a job that gives you expression and room for promotion, that sort of thing. Use it when you're looking, to see what's out there. If you have too many options, use it again to help you choose. Then use it when you're applying and then again after the interview. That's a lot of magick for one sigil so you can use it less if you want, but that multi-pronged attack is said to work really well.

Attract a Job That Suits Your Needs

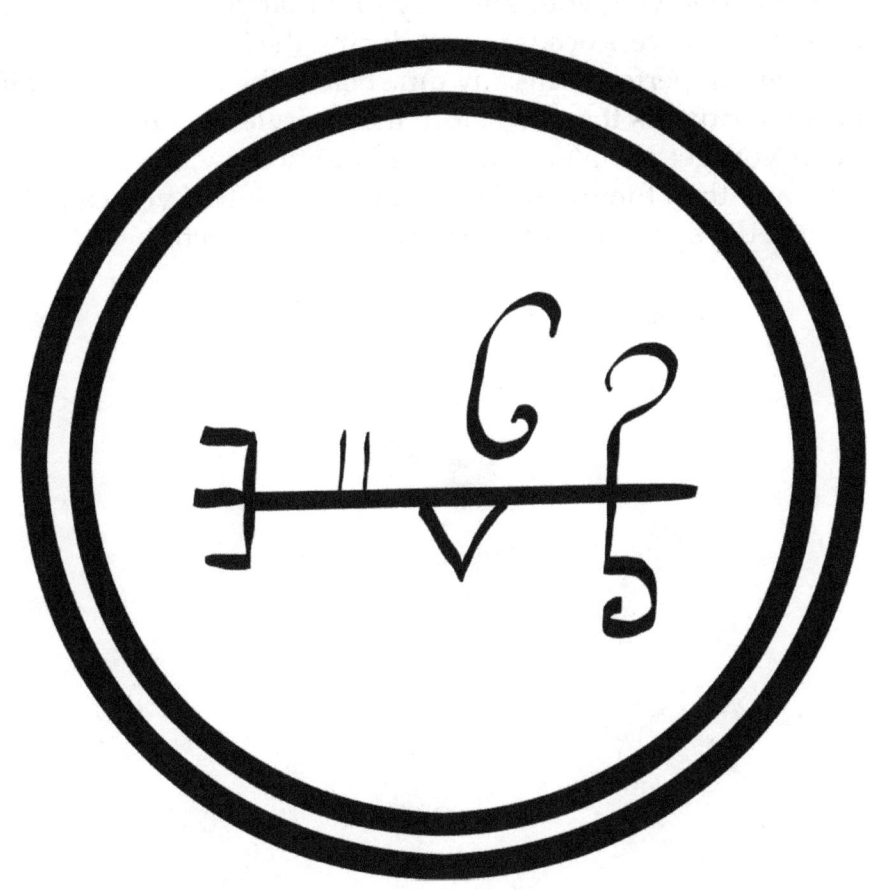

Perform Well at Interview

This sigil isn't just about improving your performance at the interview but helps you to be seen honestly and clearly by the person interviewing you. You may find that you are calm, and that perfect answers occur to you during the interview.

You can perform this any time before the interview, but if your final ritual is the day before the interview, that's the best way. If you get an interview and it's tomorrow, do the ritual today, and then tomorrow before the interview if you can. It's not three days, but it's still going to have an effect.

Perform Well at Interview

Be Noticed by People of Importance

If you perceive somebody as important – that is, important to you and your future - this sigil can make sure you don't go unnoticed. In large meetings, group gatherings, or even one on one (when there's a risk the other person will just dismiss you), this gives you a charismatic edge that gets you noticed and listened to.

Be Noticed by People of Importance

Communicate Clearly

Use this sigil when you're communicating one on one, and you need to be heard clearly. This doesn't mean you'll sway the other person to agree with you, but it means you'll be understood, and your ideas won't be clouded through poor communication. It works in relationships and with strangers. I find this one works well if the ritual is completed minutes before a meeting or discussion. But it can also be used more generally so that you communicate clearly with a specific person over a longer period of time. If there's more than one person you want to communicate with, repeat the ritual for each person, or consider the next sigil.

Communicate Clearly

Communicate to a Group

The same power as the previous sigil, but this works for groups. If you want to convince a room full of people, or at least get them to hear your message, use this sigil. Like the previous sigil, this doesn't actually make people fall under the spell of your message but makes sure people listen and understand you clearly. It's great for public speaking too.

If you don't know when a particular meeting will happen, then just sweeten communication between yourself and the group in a quite general way. If you know exactly when the meeting is, it might be an idea to target that exact meeting.

Sometimes it works well if you combine it with the previous sigil. Say you're in a business meeting or even a family gathering, and you want everybody to understand, but most of all you want to convince the *main decision-maker* – then it's great to use both sigils.

Communicate to a Group

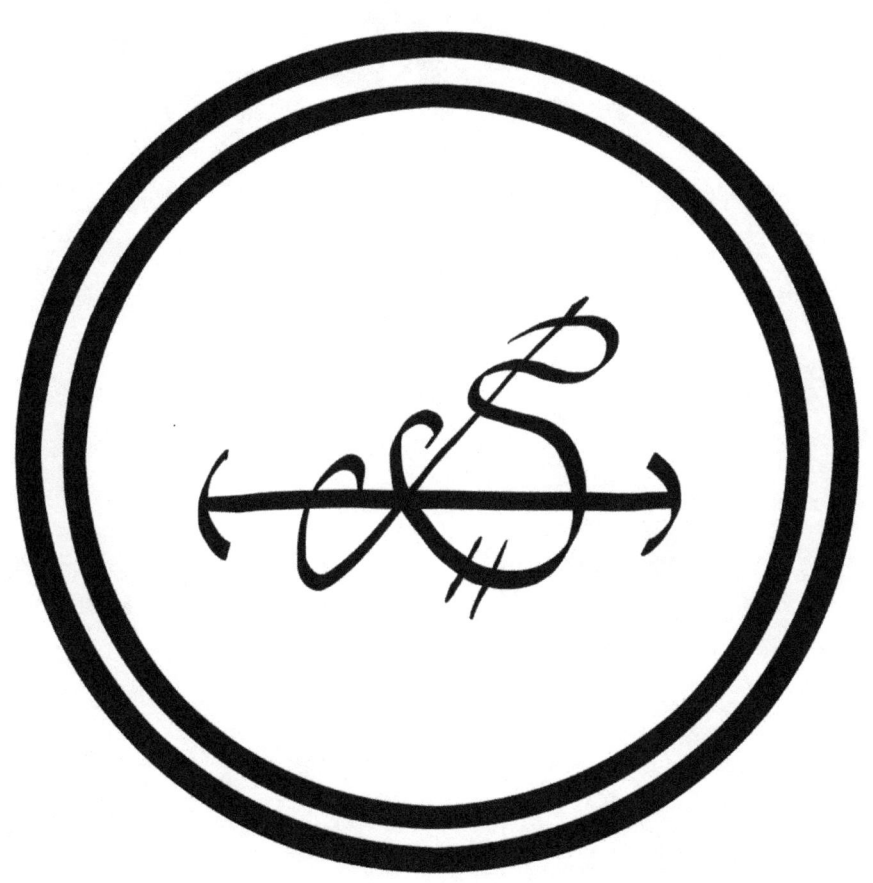

End Notes

There's one last tip I want to give you. ***If in doubt, try it out.*** Magick that stays in a book is wasted magick. If you get the feeling that magick *might* work, it only takes a small investment of time and effort, and you will see your magickal skills develop and the results begin to flow. That's what I want for you.

The sigils are not designed to be amulets. My definition of amulet is something that you wear or carry around with you, in the hope that it has a magickal effect. That's not what these sigils are for, but it's not going to do any harm. If you're going to a job interview and want to have a copy of the interview sigil somewhere on your person, be my guest. It might help. The only reason I don't mention this in the main part of the book is that I don't want you to think you *have* to do a lot of photographing, printing, and cutting out, with stacks of sigils hidden around your home (or smuggled into your clothing). This is not a book you're meant to cut up. The sigils work in the book. But if you really feel the need to have a copy with you, it might help, and it won't do any harm. If you're happy using the simple method, where the sigil stays in the book, I'm happy too!

You can make copies of the sigils, and even make jewelry based on the images, but this can only be for personal use and not for resale of any kind. When creating personal copies, you are free to photocopy, photograph or take screenshots and print them out. Such copies may not be shared with others. You are also free to draw your own sigils based on those in the book, so long as they are for personal use.

You may not reproduce these images commercially or to share with others. A book such as this takes many years to prepare and is costly to produce. Even the eBook is expensive to distribute; we get charged for every image, and the clearer the image, the more it costs us. Did you know that lots of publishers make their images smaller and fuzzier, to make more profit? I refuse to do that, and I include the sigils at full size and clarity, so you get your money's worth, even though it puts a big cut in my royalty. What's the point in using visual magick if you can't see what you're looking at?

This really has been a massive undertaking for me, so if you like the book, please write a review. I am always pleased to hear that magick is working out for you, so thank you in advance.

If you have any problems or challenges, there are FAQs on our website, and I bet you can find out anything you need to know there. New ideas are posted on the site every few weeks, to keep your magick alive.

If you have an interest in developing your magick further, there are many texts that can assist you.

The 72 Sigils of Power by Zanna Blaise covers Contemplation Magic (for insight and wisdom) and Results Magic (for changing the world around you). She is also the author of *The Angels of Love*, which can heal relationships and attract a soulmate. (She's produced an album of New Age orchestral music called *An Echo of Angels*, and it's stunning.)

Words of Power and *The Greater Words of Power* present an extremely simple ritual practice, for bringing about change in yourself and others, as well as directing and attracting changed circumstances. *Mystical Words of Power* takes this style of magick to the highest level.

For those seeking more money, *Magickal Cashbook* uses a ritual to attract small bursts of money out of the blue, and works best when you are not desperate, but when you can approach the magick with a sense of enjoyment and pleasure. *Magickal Riches* is more comprehensive, with rituals for everything from gambling to sales, with a master ritual to oversee magickal income. For the more ambitious, *Wealth Magick* contains a complex set of rituals for earning money by building a career. For those still trying to find their feet, there is *The Magickal Job Seeker*.

Magickal Protection contains rituals that can be directed at specific problems, as well as a daily practice called The Sword Banishing, which is one of our most popular and effective rituals. For those who cannot find peace through protection, there is *Magickal Attack*, by Gordon Winterfield. Dark magick is not to everybody's taste, but this is a highly moral approach that puts the emphasis on using authority to restore peace.

Magickal Seduction is a text that looks at attracting others by using magick to amplify your attractive qualities, rather than through deception. *Adventures in Sex Magick* is a more specialized text, for those open-minded enough to explore this somewhat extreme form of magick.

The Master Works of Chaos Magick is an overview of self-directed and creative magick, which also includes a section covering the Olympic Spirits. *Magickal Servitors* takes another aspect of Chaos Magick and updates it into a modern, workable method.

The 72 Angels of Magick is a comprehensive book of angel magick, and explores hundreds of powers that can be applied by working with these angels. *The Angels of Alchemy* works with 42 angels for personal transformation, which can be the key to unlocking magick.

Archangels of Magick by Damon Brand is the most comprehensive book of magick we have published, covering sigils, divination, invocation, and evocation.

There are many posts on the website that help with magick, and it's the best place to find out more. I hope to see you there.

Adam Blackthorne

www.galleryofmagick.com

CPSIA information can be obtained
at www.ICGtesting.com
Printed in the USA
LVHW032257240120
644780LV00001B/19